Poems and Prose
A Little Bit of This, A Little Bit of That

William Mijo Granich

Copyright © 2017 William Mijo Granich
Published by
Bamboo Entertainment, Inc.
4607 Lakeview Canyon Road Suite 181
Westlake Village, CA 91361

All rights reserved. No part of this book may be reproduced in whole or in part without written permission from the publisher, except by reviewers who may quote brief excerpts in connection with a review in a newspaper, magazine, or electronic publication; not may any part of this book be reproduced, stored in a retrieval system, or transmitted in any for or by any means electronic, mechanical, photocopying, recording, or other, without written permission from the publisher.
ISBN: 978-1-883212-29-2

INTRODUCTION

William Mijo Granich was born in Eureka, California in 1923. This book is a collection of poems and prose that he wrote over a span of many years. They were inspired by the many places he visited, and people he met, and also by his own creative imagination.

A Child's Prayer Overheard

Dear Lord, I want to thank Mr. Bennie Factor for what he did for my family. I don't know him but I heard my mommy and daddy say he is keeping the wolf away from our front door until my daddy gets a job. But I like the wolf, he's so fluffy and nice. Tell him to come to the back door some time. We don't have much food but I'll feed him some of mine.

And also dear Lord, if you can remember, please send me a stitch. My mommy says a stitch in time will save nine. I don't know what a stitch is but my daddy likes them because when he laughs watching television he says he is in stitches and I don't want him to run out of them.

Oh, and could you please make our grass a little greener. I only ask this because I hear the grass is greener in the next pasture and I want ours to be as good as theirs. Yes and please send the cat away once in awhile cause mommy says that when the cat's away the mouse will play and I would like to play with him.

So now I must lay me down to sleep and pray my soles you will keep dry because I will need them when I walk to school tomorrow. Daddy said our luck is so bad that it never rains but it pours and I don't want my feet to get wet. But that's not so bad though, because when they get wet and I sneeze everyone says "Bess you" and I like that because my name is Elizabeth and a lot of people call me Bess and I like that a lot.

Amen.

A Conversation re: Life

If I knew what life was going
To bring – I'd probably reject it.

But how would you do that,
    They said,
    And still be here?
Oh, I'd still be here, but I'd
    Move move and not leave a
    Forwarding address.

Then it would end up in the unclaimed section of life,
    Wouldn't it?
    They asked.
I'm sure it would – but
    That's life,
    That's part of living.

Then how could you go on?

Oh, I'd take on a new persona,
    A new identity.
I'm not sure who I'd want
    To be.

That's odd, just last week
I heard someone say
They wished they had your life,
They wished they could be like you.
Really, gosh, their life must really be dull.
I can't think of anyone I'd
    Want to be.

You mean you'd be different
    Than anyone else?
Yes, I would and I'd be happy
    Being it.
Well, doesn't that make you
    Different than anyone else?

You know, I believe you're right
I am different than anyone else.
And you know what,
I think I'm happy being so.

So I don't know what life is
Going to bring, but bring it on,
I'm looking forward to it.

A Fork in Life's Road

Some people's passions turn out to create a felony
While others just want to create a melody.
It's a snake they want to charm
And feel it would do them no harm.

When one's thoughts are masked from the truth
And their soul sinks in the darkness of solitude
Those thoughts that enter their sphere
Are evil and ones they try to conceal
They are as devious as those unspoken vows
Taken between the devil and their own furrowed brows.

But there is no gain to be had
No premium bestowed on being bad.
They would in all ways better be served

To open their hearts and be heard.

The spirits are there to listen to all
To reach out and hold them before the fall,
So when they reach that fork in life's road,
The one faced by many before in
Wrestling with life's code,
They need no signposts to point them to their destination
The righteous path will always lead them in the right direction

A Friend

A friend is more than gold
Or something to borrow.

You can squander one
Or return the other tomorrow.

But a friend is yours to have and hold
and cherish beyond all tomorrows.

A Glimpse of Love

Isn't it sad
How you can lose something you never had?
Or how you can miss someone new
You never really knew?
This happened with you
When I saw you on the avenue
Our eyes met by chance
It was just a fleeting glance, but
I felt a bolt from above
Like the crashing of love.

How could it have been so quick?
You touched my heart to the wick.
Before I could even think
You disappeared in a wink.
You were lost in the crowd,
I was left alone in a cloud

Now my days are spent wondering
My nights are spent pondering,
Why is my heart so dead?

Are you the one I was destined to wed?

As the days and nights go by
And I'm alone with my memory of love,
I know I can truly buy
The theory of love at first sight.

From out of the blue
You appeared in my life.
You are the one I knew
Was destined to be my life.

If love has any powers divine
And the spirits can show pity,
Our lives will cross again in this lonely city,
And I will be yours and you will be mine.

A House Or A Home

Once I was known as a full-fledged home
Because I had family inside me.
A house needs a family to make it a home.

Now I'm empty and my rooms bare
And for me no one seems to care.

There is a house up the street aways
It's an investment and known as just a rental.
It is known as 22-7-oh-7 Myrtle
With occupants coming and going
And no family settling in to stay.

I'm known as the brown house on the corner with white shutters
I hope I don't become just a rental
And be known like them as a house with numbers.

Now my rooms are empty and my basement bare.
No cars in my garage, no lawnmower or tools hanging there.

My children grew up in me and finished the local schools.
Went off to college to learn more of society's rules.
My adults kept saying I was too big for just the two of them
So it was time to sell, move on and begin anew again.

I think back now when we first came together

POEMS AND PROSE

I was on a mortgage with a loan from the bank.
My deed of trust was held by them in a vault.
But after years I was all paid up
And a mortgage burning party was the result.

Neighbors came and celebrated the big occasion
I remember it was a happy celebration.

And I remember kids playing in my backyard and having races
Making mud pies and forts and hiding in different places.
My adults would have their friends over for barbeque outings.
Bridge parties in the living room,
Babies crawling, my carpet keeping their knees from getting sore,
Then taking their first steps right here on my floor.

My lawn was always neatly mowed and trimmed
Unlike those rentals where a truck drives up to its yard.
Workers jump out and mow, blow, and go before they are even tired.

My adult tried hiring help with the lawn one time.
Got that terrible Eddie from up the street
Whose work was not worth even one dime.
Told him to cut my grass first this way and then that
And to be sure to trim the edges
'Cause that makes it nice to see.
Well he sure hustled us like a pro and you can believe me
Missed cutting a spot, or two or three.
Didn't even bother to trim the edges
Nor even swept the walk as far as I could see.
Well from then on my adult did it all himself believe me.

Now I'm alone and waiting patiently
For adults to climb my front stairs to look and see
As they follow the salesperson who always has the key
Ask questions about my foundation, plumbing and electricity
And invariably ask how many square feet there are in me.
While their children sit in the car and wait
Their noses pressed to the cars' windows and about to salivate

I'll bet if they ran through my rooms just once
They would tell their parents that I'm the one
In which they want their beds to bounce.

But wait, there's a car stopping right outside my front door.
It's a mom and pop and little kids I could adore.

I see two, three, no I can count four
And they're all getting out the car's doors.
The adults are smiling and shaking hands with the sales agent.

I've seen them before, yes it was just a week ago.
I liked them a whole lot then and hated to see them go.
The bigger kid is smiling and saying with joy,
"Oh, daddy this is really great, really great, oh boy!"
For me this is what it is all about.
I'm so happy hearing this I could shout.
You know this may be my lucky day.
This may be my family who will settle down and stay.
The family who will change me from just a house and into a home.

A Pile of Words

They are just a pile of words
thrown in a heap.
Like a cord of wood cut and
ready to keep.
My task is to find the ones
with caring and meaning,
Like you and us, together and must,
Like love and lust and even those
cautious in meaning.
Let go and dare, hold tight and delight.
Sort them out and stack them and
view them in their true light.
Find the ones that mean I love you,
I need you, I truly do.
Hold me and caress me, strip the words
to their true meaning.
Bare and undress them, those
cloaked in caution and misleading.
Strip them of doubt, disrobe them to
what they are about.
From this pile of words reveal their
true meaning, so as to warm
ourselves from our hearts to our toes
Enough to carry over into our souls.

Add Up the Lights of Shooting Stars

The moment was captured in my heart

And repeats and repeats itself when we are apart.
Like a staccato of flashes from shooting stars
Whose combined lights shine on my memory so distant and dark.

When first we met we followed the rules of etiquette
And would part with a courteous hug and a brush of us.
But that one time when almost by chance we did connect
And felt the warm glow of the dawn of love
Our lips momentarily found each other's hungry longing for delight,
Like two shooting stars rushing to kiss the earth that night.

That moment was the first flash of life to come.
Flashes that would combine to a total light
Like shooting stars of an entire galaxy.
A light that would forever illuminate our lives
And make us what we are today.
Lovers and friends and partners from here to the end.

Be Happy

Worry, anguish, fretting and tears
Take their toll over the years.
On that you can bet
And it's one you won't regret.

Smile, laugh and be happy
Does you a world of good instead
No need to bet on that
Just look around and you'll understand.

Once I knew a man who was all frowns,
Didn't care for any of the world around,
Denied himself all the happiness
And ended only with loneliness.

But the one that was always smiling
Going from friend to friend enjoying
Was the one everyone wanted around
For he was a friend they all could surround.

Be Yourself At Your Best

Ask not why you are not wealthy
Understand why you are not poor.

WILLIAM MIJO GRANICH

Ask not why you are not happy
Understand why you do not brood.

Ask not why you are not a leader
Understand why you follow your chosen path.

Material items one can sort and count
Spiritual wealth is inventoried in the heart.

Ask not why you are not another
Understand who you are and what will make you better.

Be Yourself

He aspired to be a great poet, a dreamer of dreams.
So he rented a house adjacent to a great poet whose
commonality was their alley of trash cans.

Each week he diligently availed himself of his neighbor's
discarded notes before the trash collectors carted them away.

This was his treasured source of dreams
even though they were not his own.

For years on end he wrote verse on verse
from his prized collection,
all the while jealously admiring his neighbor's success
of dreams expressed by words in print.

Then came the day his words were ready to be printed for display.
The next morning the trash collectors
on their routine round carted his life's work away.
And at that moment he became the man he dreamt to be.

The moral is you cannot steal another man's dreams
and hope to be what you are not.
Fulfill your own dreams and be what is your lot
And that could be more than what you thought.

Because I Care

I'm a big, brown, lonely
Grizzly bear

Lying on the hill looking
Down at you.

The clearing that you're in,
The picnic basket full of
Goodie things laid out
All caught my eye,
And make my feelings come alive.

Enjoy the sun, emjoy the sky
I'll look after you.
No hunter in the woods,
No walkers on the trail,
Will even come close
To entering your world.

I'll scare them off,
I'll make them go around
Your picnic spot.
I wish you knew
How much I cared.

Captured Love

Is it practice that I need
Or is it patience I must heed?

Your love to me is so intense
My love pales in comparison.

I've never honed its cutting edge
Or tried to whet its appetite.

I've gone through the motions of caring
And even shown some outright daring.

But when your love penetrated my heart
I knew right then what was to be my part.

To include you in my whole life through
And keep your love captive in my heart so true.

WILLIAM MIJO GRANICH

Chart the Journey to Love

I don't know which way to turn to be closer to you.
Where on earth to search to end my sadness.
I only know to end my blue
I need to find you and stop this madness.

If I were a compass I'd have a magnetic clue.
My needle would point in the direction of you.
If I were a hound dog searching around
I'd pick up your trail and I know you'd be found.

An adventurist I could be and search the entire earth,
Travel from here to Mozambique and back,
Turn around and head for places I don't even know exist
And as there is a heaven above in my search I must persist.

Sometimes I feel the path I'm on is divine.
And then I feel it is just a matter of time.
Then as I am close to you it seems
I awake and find it was only a dream.

Navigators chart their courses by the stars
They include planets like Jupiter and Mars.
They know their objective, their destinations
And reach their conclusions without hesitation.

But the chart that would take me directly to you
Could only be chartered by dreams that come true.

I dream of the time I will hold you in my arms
And know that you are mine, all mine.
Dream of nights we walk under the stars
Holding hands and knowing that what we have is true love
While all the planets and stars smile on us from above.

Choices

If I had to choose
You can bet I would not lose.

A poor man would choose wealth,
A rich man would choose health.

A farmer would choose rain,

Yet his crop could go down the drain.

The world would choose peace,
But a mouse would choose cheese.

A ballerina would choose applause
Yet the audience may not feel her cause.

So between health and wealth,
applause and peace

I say let the mouse have his cheese.

Everyone must choose what they feel is true.
My choice is very simple, of all the world,
I choose you.

Containment

My mind contains the thoughts of you.
My heart contains my love so true.

My arms reach out to make you mine.
Your heart and mind reach out so as to define

The parameters of entertainment,
The ecstasy of containment.

Our lips are contained with tender touch,
Our bodies entwine with a gentle rush.

Lying here in the morning light,
My love reflecting in your eyes so bright,
Recalls to me the joy of last night,
The passions unleashed with pure delight.

My thoughts are not restricted by convention,
My actions are the result of invention.

I care not what the world thinks of my lament,
I care only of you and me embraced in complete containment.

WILLIAM MIJO GRANICH

Contentment

A contented man needs no bookmark
as he reads from his book of life,
for to re-read a few pages
relives his enjoyment of what he once
thought was past and so reaches
a higher apogee of content.

Danitsa, The Morning Star
or
Is It Fantasy

Danitsa, Danitsa, moya draga slatka Danica.
My dear, sweet Danica,
You appear in the morning light
As though in fantasy,
But as the day goes bright
You fade away in the galaxy.

I murmur your name
To the lilt of sweet refrain.
I long for your sight
So my heart can take flight.

To fly toward you, the star in the sky,
Away, away, in the sky so high.
But as you fade away,
I'm destined to wait another day.

After waiting through another night so dark
My heart is ready to embark.
Waiting for the morning light,
Hoping to reach you on its next lonely flight.

Dark Moments

Most of us have dark moments in our lives.
So we choose not to expose those of others.
Not out of gallantry or charity,
But from fear that our own dark moments
will be exposed under the
scrutiny of investigative glare.

They could be ill-gotten satisfactions of
hidden lusts secreted away,
Or dark moments hidden under the
cloak of good manners.
Or self-serving gains illegally grabbed
by those in authority.
Who in turn are shielded by their lessers
who have desires of their own similar gains.
Many of these silences at times come
under the heading of civilization.
If you do not have dark moments in
your life maybe you haven't lived long enough.

Or if your dark moments can be exposed
to the light of truth and you can withstand
the consequences of their scrutiny, then you are
rare among men and are blessed with
a conscience that is pure and at peace.

Do Dream On

What is this vision before me,
this form I make out to be?

Is it partially dressed
Or is my mind just stressed?

Is it a dream collage
Or is my appetite too large?

Is it a mannequin?
but then I should look again.

If I open my eyes
Will it crystallize?

Or will it vanish into air
And leave me standing here?

Should I offer it myself,
What if it demands much more?

What if it wants my flesh
And it is not satisfied with less?

Can I pass the test of amour?
I can see it has real glamour.

Should I reach out to touch its flesh
Or control my wants and not be selfish?

Oh well my wants are pure and simple
Eeny, meany, miney, moe,
Where is its dimple?

Don't Strike Out In Life

How many times have you heard this before?
But stop me if it seems a big bore.
His wife done him wrong
And that he could put to a song.

His best friend was unwitting
But she knew a lot of tricking
Now what would it take
To resolve this for goodness sake?
A bullet through the head
Or good riddance instead?
But why waste his time
And besides he's not into crime?

As wives go she was OK
But as his kids' mother
He wouldn't want any other.
And now she gave him a chance at a new life
And then again maybe a new wife.
Now there are new rules to the game
And in some ways he's not to blame.
Now that the kids are grown and gone
He can feel the important work is done.

He is now the alpha spouse
And of course he'll give her the house.
His ace in the hole is he's still young enough,
Just pull himself together
And show the world he's tough.

A new phase in his life is beginning.
So give it his best shot and prosper in living.

Dreams

Before you appeared on the scene
My life was just a dull dream.
Life was simple it did appear,
Scheduled to go on year after year.

Small talk with friends,
A golf game that never ends.
Meals taken without company,
Lonely walks in the country.

Movies shared with no one,
Watching games on TV until they're done.
Having no idea who won,
No idea even after the rerun.

Then you came into town.
What was my permanent frown
Turned into a smile and laughter.
I knew then what I was really after.

You hold the key to my future dreams.
You even control my hopes.
My frowns are now smiles that beam,
I feel I am no longer a dope.

This duty do not take lightly,
The results I will see nightly.
My dreams will be my part,
You be careful as you hold my heart.

Endless Nights, Endless Days

Ever since you went away
My sleepless nights will never end.
I pray I'll make it through the night
Though I can't bear to face the light of day.

You said it was time for us to wed,
I chose that we should wait instead.
How did I know that my delay
Would cause you to turn your head and stray?

I never knew what I had
I never cared if you were good or bad.
My life was happy both night and day.
My world was to enjoy and play.

Now I lie alone and lonely in my bed.
It's the nights that I so dread.
I lie awake and toss all night,
Knowing I was wrong and you were right.
I count the hours for the night to end,
Knowing my heart will never mend.

When the morning light shines through the dark,
My misery shifts from sleepless nights to troubled days.
I count the pieces of my broken heart
And wish the world would just go away.

Without you at my side
I want to set the world aside.
I pray I'll make it through the day
And the nights and days somehow to go away.

My life now is such a lark,
I'm just an actor who hits his mark.
Going through life with all the motions
With no sign of any real emotions.

My life blends into one huge blob,
Days are nights and nights are days it's plain.
Time is measured by my heart's throb.
I pray I'll make it through the pain.

Ever since you went away,
My life is lonely in every way
Ever since we were not to wed,
I pray I'll make it through the end.

Faith

You don't have to be introduced to God,
You can meet him all by yourself.
God has no secretary – just dial Him direct.
1-800 and you won't have to pay a cent.

I've talked to Him, mostly at night,

But he'll always listen, especially if you're uptight.
Prayers are not answered in the order received,
It depends if you have faith and what you really need.

So give Him a try and call Him yourself.
It may be new to you and seem different at first.
But once you make that connection
It's a number you'll never forget.

Fantasy

I wish that we could be alone
in some place faraway
Like Timbuktoo or Mandalay
So that I could reveal my
lust and fantasies and love for you.

But under the stark, harsh reality
of life, this cannot be.
This cannot be for now or ever be.
So I must lock up my
wants and desires and my love for you.
Fantasies of legs and arms and bodies entwined,
Minds shared and emotions and love
that would form our glowing life.
Seal them up in my heart along with
my dreams of you and me
And keep them secret from now to the end.

And as I'm lying alone and lonely
in the dark night of life
I can unlock my wants
and cravings and love for you
and let my secrets free to dance
With me from now until we can be.

Feelings

A poem is not just a few chosen words well written.
It takes life when the poets senses are smitten
And feel the tug on the strings of their hearts
As the breezes waft through their innermost thoughts
And stir and rustle feelings of their days and nights,

As their lives behold the golden dawn unfold
To a wonderous world of new and old.

But not all thoughts are of glee and joy
Some tell of pangs of the heart and disarray
And sadly recount the feelings of hurt and pain.
Some appear fresh and new and still damp from the morning rain.
Others show signs of tears and long felt emotions and fears
Secreted away and stored in the heart for years.

But what is primarily and vastly important
Is the feelings were recorded and not left to lie dormant.
For they then become a piece of one's self,
Recorded in the giant tabloid of life
And left to others to read and to decipher.
Or like rain on the windshield of strife
To just apply the wipers.

Forbidden Love

Let us part with this sweet, sweet goodbye,
By lighting the flame on our candle of love.
And for just a minute warm our souls with its flickering glow
While we reflect on our so few hours of tender, wild, unbridled love.

Then as we hold each other tightly,
Snuff out the flame with our silent tears,
And let our candle of love stand
Coldly as a silent witness to our secret hours.
The forbidden hours when in our embrace
You were as I and I as you
And we both knew this too
Would come to an end.

Forever Love

Many theories abound of how the world evolved.
There are also countless discussions which also involve
Of when the feeling of beauty and love was first detected
and whom were the first to be so affected
I join such discussions with my own theory
That each of us is his own judge and jury
In deciding their fate in matters of the heart
And how it all comes about right from the start

It could happen in a matter of moments
While pursuing dreams of sheer contentment
Just listen to the case I lay out for you
And tell me if you feel my theory could be true.

There upon the silky sheets she lay
Her beauty in pure and wondrous display
Her aura of innocence filled the air
As though an angel was lying there
As her deflowered petals lay upon my heart
I knew the answer we both had sought
She was now the dedication for my life
The beginning of forever love that seemed so right

A soldier of fortune I am not
A prisoner of love is now my lot
My theory is pure and utterly simple
And need not be solved as a complex riddle
For they who have never thirsted for love
Are not worthy to love or to be loved.

Goodnight My Love

Goodnight my love for now you must sleep.
Sleep my love and dream ,oh so deep.

Dream my love, dream of me,
For I will surely dream of thee.

Sleep and dream, dream what can be,
Just you and me, our love
     lasting for eternity.

Here's Looking at You Babe

Lately I've had this recurring exciting dream.
It includes you my dear and Bailey's Irish Cream.
This drink I'm sure was meant to be served in a glass,
But I started to think: Wouldn't it be better on a lass?
Bailey's Irish Cream poured on you,
Now that's my choice of drink it's true.

There are many containers from which to drink,
A cup or glass, a pitcher, or alas, a saucer you'd think.

But a navel as a vessel you say,
For this I'll settle with a grand hooray.

We'll toast us to a skol or cheers or bottoms up,
But then it would spill from you 'cause you're not built like a cup.

Lie still and don't move,
To pour is just the start,
I just know you will approve
To drink will be my part.

You may not hold a full ounce,
And please try not to bounce.
You'll be the ultimate prop,
I hope to drink without spilling a drop.

You just give me the cue
I'll drink to you on you.
I'll drink to my heart's content
And forever cherish this exciting moment.

Here's looking at you, babe,
As you lie still and unabashed.
Here's drinking to you, babe,
I just hope I don't get smashed.

Hold the Presses

I thought the pages of my life were neatly writ and nearly filled, ready to put away.
If not, the ones to go were reserved for what I thought was real.
Then along came you with all your caring and charms.
Who would have known your type was so thrilling and so, so real?
Who would have guessed life could still be a big deal?
It forced me to open my book of life along with my heart,
And start penning all sort of romantic stuff.
Now I can share and experience all types of things.
New ones and old ones and the old ones are now something.

You put a spin on my life that I thought was nearly complete,
But now is just the start of happiness replete.
Now I need to fill more pages of you and me,
And am even planning a brighter cover, you'll see.

Now I feel my book of life is being written anew.
And on its way to the best-sellers list as it features you.

The main character about which my life now revolves,
The angel sent to me from the very heavens above.

How Wrong Is My Love For You

How wrong can you be if you love someone?
How wrong can you be to do what they want?
When you said actions speak louder than words,
My words were all about my love for you.
My actions are something I did not understand.
So how wrong could I have been to do what I did?
How wrong could I have been if my love was all for you?

Now you found another.
Someone you say you love.
I can't find another love
'Cause my love is all used up over you.
I get confused when I talk to others.
I can't understand where actions take the place of words.
My words are now hollow and blue
'Cause my heart was used up by my love for you.

I Am Not But Want To Be

You make me what I am not
But want to be a lot.

Yesterday a man so overwrought with flesh
Asked my opinion of his weight
Knowing my answer could hurt his pride
I took his question in full stride.

Before I met you without hesitation I would have replied:
You are fat and your diet must not be delayed.
But you brought out the diplomat in me and I said:
Your build is strong and admired a lot my friend.

This past week while strolling through the town
Sirens blared to signal a building burning down.
As there was no fireman or volunteer around
Quick as a flash with you in mind
I ran the stairs, the flames making a terrible sound.
Heard a poor soul screaming for aid
His rescue was attributed to me they said.

While walking in the park I saw a man drowning in the lake.
Quick as a wink and thinking of you
Without a moment lost and my clothes not shed,
I swam the lake to reach him in time,
Had him on the shore for the paramedics to do the rest.

The other night in a cold and icy stream
A dog was being washed away to its doom it seemed.
As it was struggling and thrashing to save its hide
With no one in sight I ran the bank in full stride.
Jumped to the center of the stream and swam like a shark.
The cold water was churning and dark, I could hardly hear the dog bark.
Back on the bank his tail did wag
As he licked my hands while lying limp as a rag.

This alone was reward enough for me
As I thought of you and the magic I could see.

Was it hero or crisis or rising to the task
I never felt so before and now of you I ask
Please my love from my life do not stray.
You made a man of me and so I pray
Stay in my newfound life of love
And make me what I am not but want to be.
This newfound love of life and people and things
That is what you are making of me,
And it is everything I want to be.

I Can't Deny Love

My life has been one long denial, not of truth or fact
But denial of happiness, comfort, and in fact
All that is bestowed on an infant at birth
The right to a good life for all that it's worth.

You came into my life just in time,
To allow me to see what was rightfully mine.
You opened my eyes to the truth and fact
That life was here for me to take and react
To all your giles and charms
And for me to take you in my arms,
To hold and to cherish 'til heaven above
Gives me the signal that this is not denial but true love.

I Gambled and Lost

My feelings for you run so deep
I find I lie in bed and cannot sleep.
Your impression on me is so indelible
I can only think of it as incredible.

Not only did you sweep me off my feet,
I learned that in every victory there is also defeat.
Some win, some lose, but this time it wasn't even close.
With my luck you are the one I chose.

Heads you win, tails I lose.
Is that the formula you choose?
Why do you insist on playing this game?
Long ago I tossed in my chips in vain.

In the contest of life you play
The cards are all stacked your way.
In this little game you seem so contrite,
But that doesn't make wrong into right.

I wasn't gambling for fortune or fame,
I wasn't even hoping to change your name.
My chips are all spent,
My heart is broken and bent.

My wish that we be together in good health
Is just another losing hand I was dealt.
My wish that we would never part,
Was just the setting to break my heart.

My love that was so sweet is now full of sorrows,
Destined to go on for endless tomorrows.

I'm tired of this game,
My heart is filled with pain.
My feelings for you still run deep
Now my love I must lie down and pray I sleep.

WILLIAM MIJO GRANICH

I Reached for the Stars

I was guilty of reaching for the stars,
I felt you were part of the galaxy.
To reach you would be easier if I lived on Mars.
The thought of holding you was real audacity.

I was the victim of my imagination.
Instead of using my knowledge of celestial navigation,
Trying to reach the stars with my heart
Was entertaining trouble and tearing me apart.

Seeing you in all my dreams and thoughts
Was just the formula I had sought.
But as I look back to figure where I went wrong,
It was that I trusted life as if it were a song,
A song set to a rhythmical beat and measure,
But your role in life made it more a treasure.

You once were a princess in her court,
Now you are the Queen we all support.
You set the rules to which we play,
Just as the Queen bee as she flies away.
The worker bees lay down their chores
And fly to join the Queen as their retort.

I understand the rules we must follow
As I am one who cherishes the
     prospects of tomorrow.

The rules you lay down are simple and clear.
You need your space, solitude, and atmosphere.

Worker bees must tune into your needs.
And respect your wishes with noble deeds.
For it is only then when I reach for a star,
Will I be happy even though I know
     it is very, very far.

POEMS AND PROSE

I Searched for You

I love you for loving me.
You make me glad for being me.

I never kept a diary,
Or mementos from a date,
But always wondered how life would be
If I could find my mate.

And now I know and truly believe,
I loved you before we even met.

You make my life so real,
That I will never forget
You and life are a treat.
Finding you makes me complete.

I Want My Brand on You

The cowboy brands his horse
But then sets it free on its course.

The farmer tills and plants his field
For the crop he raises is his yield.

The mezzo soprano fills the air
With a beautiful sonata with delicate care.

The prospector dams a river to find gold
But later turns it loose before he's too old.

The young man, the old man, the woman and girl
All have their dreams to give them a goal.

My thoughts are the brand that only I imagine,
For I want you to be free and then you can think of me.

Yours is an excitement no man should harness,
Your mind, your thoughts, your world, must always illuminate the darkness.

WILLIAM MIJO GRANICH

I'm a Bronco Bustin' Cowboy

My Mama wanted me to be a dentist,
My Papa said a lawyer be,
As a boy I was torn between the two
'Cause I loved them both you see.

but then along came Aunt Emily,
My uncle's second wife he left to make it three.
She really made up my mind for me
She taught me all the things to make a man of me.
A bronco bustin' cowboy I would end up to be.

There's nothing she didn't know,
She really prepared me for the show.
She taught me how to mount and dismount without using the saddle horn.
It felt so good I wished I had known it from the day I was born.
She taught me not to hurry but just hang on and enjoy the ride.
If I ever got thrown from that filly once we were in stride,
I knew I had to remount or it would really hurt my pride.

For days on end and many nights into the blue
We practiced, the two of us, in secret solitude.

This was the life for me, this life so free.
This bronco bustin' business was my cup of tea.
Sometimes we practiced just off the trail,
The one that goes through the meadow and around the bend.
At times we practiced behind the corral,
All the while I hoped my tutoring would never end.

At times the hay would mat my hair,
My shirt would be sweaty and my chest bare.

Then as I grew up the years began to flow,
And I upped and joined the rodeo.
The little towns would seem to blend
      and never end,
And the seasons turned into years.
Now when I look back I see my past through dusty tears.

I'm still riding the rodeo circuit and all in vain,
For all the honky tonk stops add up to hurt and pain.

Now there's an Emily in every town,
They're not my aunts but they sure do seem to get around.
It's too late for me a dentist to be,

And as for a lawyer that also requires a degree.
I'm just a bronco bustin' cowboy, that I really know.
Destined to ride on to the end of the final show.

I'm Ready

Man can get drunk on grape,
Their minds hung down like a drape.
Man can turn into a fool
And seem to all not so cool.

I can get drunk on you
With my mind alert and true.
I then look so bright and heady,
But I really owe a lot to your teddy.

Ice Candles

My soul has wandered in search of you its mate.
But my search has wavered from its path of late.
Some stumbles, some missteps, some indiscretions which I now regret.

But in my heart I've always known
My life is an ice candle whose flame
glows with the burning of my soul.

Ever since we met I knew my
candle would not melt in waste.
But thrive and float in the clouds until it mends.
To light our path to forever happiness
from now until the end.

Identify the Quarry

Have you ever wondered what your conduct meant?
Especially at the distaff end.
Are you a gentleman of good repute
Or one of dissolute and lacking resolute?
Maybe even a scoundrel absolute?

Are you no better than a courser

Whose dogs are your guileful charms?
Whose braying and cunning alarms
Unsuspecting maidens to seek haven in your arms?

Is it your intent to deflower your quarry?
Those wide-eyed creatures of beauty?
Are they the target of your actions
And who could possibly end up as your bounty
As their vulnerable hearts search for true love?

But be careful as your heart could suffer before it is done.
Your heart could trip upon its quarry
And tangle itself in its exploitful chase
And then hunter would be the hunted in this case.

Looking to insulate his own heart
Wondering if the chase took on a new start
Trying to straighten out his own thoughts
Wondering if the chase was about to fall apart.

If I Only Knew What Yesterday Would Bring

How can life be so wrong?
Yesterday's memories are today's fantasies.

How can life be so wrong?
Yesterday's sweet realities are today's cruel song.

How can life be so upside down?
Yesterday's smiles are today's frowns.

How can life be so inside out?
Who dictates what life is all about?

Who writes life's script and especially mine?
I don't remember giving them power divine.

If there is a plan they don't know where I belong.
My wish it that yesterday continue all along.

My only relief is when I fall asleep
The turmoil of life is not so deep.
My dreams are built on pleasant thoughts
Of yesterdays laughs and the caring we always sought.

But as I wake in fits and starts during the night
The dark reality of my life confirms my plight.
And the morning call to face life as it is now
Makes me want to crawl back into my dreams and pray for night to fall.

I never knew when we decided to part
My life would be a nightmare falling apart.
so as I face the reality of days end
I pray the day's nightmares will end
And in my dreams I will hold you tight
And love you and cherish you
Throughout the whole night.

Imagination

Was that imagination or did our
lips just brush?
Was that imagination or did our
bodies just touch?

Even now in the dark
My imagination runs stark

Oh, my friend, my love,
Be gentle as a dove.

Come fly the warm breeze,
Come fill my every need.

For you alone are my love
And I but a lonely dove.

Imagination II

Imagination is a world of its own.
Nothing can stop the imagination I own.

I can imagine everyone waking up to a puppy on their bed.
Or two people in love having the right to wed.
A horse race where everyone wins.
An eight horse race ending in a dead heat.
Peaches and cream in everyone's dish.
Rubies and diamonds as every girl's wish.

I can imagine anything happening in thiis world,
Involving people or things, or even chocolate ferris wheels.
But I can't imagine my world without you.
I can't imagine not wanting you.
I can't imagine not loving you.

In my imagination I can make my dreams come true,
Especially those dreams that always include you.
Please love me as much as I love you.
You make my imaginations come true.

It's Just So

Why do you write, the poet was asked.
Why do you breathe, he replied.

Why do you fly, the bird was asked.
Why do you dream was his reply.

Why do you swim, the fish was asked.
Why does the sun shine in the sky, he replied.

Nature is all God at rest and
All God is nature at its best.
No need for you to ask of another
their reason for being and not some other.
For it is then you will know in your heart
The reason for your being you is just your part.

Kaleidoscope

I miss you so much I ache.
My heart, my spirit, my soul are about to break.
The brief time we had together,
My thoughts I barely had time to gather.

You gave me a glimpse of what life could be,
That glimpse is indelible in my mind to me.
How can a glimpse generate into a kaleidoscope of dreams?
Dreams that I feel were meant to be.

Each time I dare think what life could be with you,
Countless multi exciting thoughts of life go off in my mind anew.

Colors burst, images appear of far away places,
And far away ideas where strangers have faces,
And places are for us to reach
If not in the mountains then down on the beach.

You control my kaleidoscope of dreams,
Your spirit presents these images in endless reams.
I'm lonely and left craving for more,
More living, more you, more me, or else life is a bore.

But just as a child tires of a toy,
You chose to put aside my kaleidoscope of dreams and end my joy.
Now I must face life in real world terms.
I must reenter my own world and never return
To a life so sweet with promise and mirth,
To cherish it for all that I'm worth.

I'm me and no more,
You're you but much more.
You control my kaleidoscope of dreams and me.
And if you choose not to turn to the next image for me to see
I must lie content with what I had
Though it was so brief, I'm not sad.
I'm stuck in this lone glimpse of what life could have been.
But it is mine, all mine, and I need not share it with anyone.

Let Love Fly Free

Let your feelings be free,
This is not about me.
Let your feelings be true,
This is about you.

Don't mask your feelings with words,
don't hide our love from the world.
And above all be aware,
A love grows because it's there.

All flowers bloom as they grow.
Corn matures row upon row.
A whale bears a calf at sea
And cares and loves it until its time comes to swim free.

Caring and loving and hurting and
    laughing are real.

But denial of love is to conceal
The true meaning of life we know,
the one thing that makes our lives glow.

Puppies are born in a litter,
But each has the instinct to love on its own.
Birds are not left alone and bitter
When hatchlings fly away to seek love on their own.

Don't dictate to your heart what it should feel
Let your heart choose the path that is real.

From an acorn an oak will grow,
From a thought a poem will flow.

Who teaches a bear love for its cub?
Who dictates the swirl of water in a tub?
Nature and life are all so real,
Love is no different though at times seems surreal.
Clouds float by for the sun to reveal,
Life and love are no different, they're real.

It doesn't take two to create love.
It could be dictated from above.
One heart is sufficient enough,
But waiting and lonely can be tough.

Let your heart fly free
And like radar at night
Will follow my heart's signals in flight,
And bring your love safely to me.

A thoroughbred is bred to cross the finish line a winner.
But its love for the race is in its heart and will always simmer.
Don't deny love and happiness within thee,
For it will cut out the life blood in me.

Like a flower that blooms in the rain forrest alone,
Nurtured by the gentle rain that sets its tone,
It doesn't bloom for the world to see,
It blooms because it is there and free.

Your love is that flower that blooms in my heart,
Nurtured by my gentle tears because we are apart.
Tears that fall gently in my heart,
And softly on the bloom in my heart.

You are a woman who blooms in love.
Don't deny yourself that feeling blessed from above.

Let our love be set free to fly,
Like a bird that soars in the sky.
Let our love be reflected in my eyes
For the world to see and realize
Two hearts can be free
though bonded by love through eternity.

Let Your Feelings Be Free

Let yourself go – let your spirit fly free.
Let your spirit be free as a bird in a tree.

Kids swing on a rope from a tree,
Then they let go and splash
in the lake and feel so free.

Moms watch their kids grow,
then they let go and their
kids are free.
Moms are that rope secured
to the tree. Kids let go
and feel free but all the while
know the security of Mom
and come back whenever they
want to splash free.

Puppies run and chase and play
oh so free. But they always
come back because they know
to be loved is to be free.

Don't be afraid to let your
spirit be free. Splash in
my lake. Swim with me.
I want to be free.

Life on the Brink

It was just a fleeting glance
Passed through a crowded room.

WILLIAM MIJO GRANICH

I knew right then it was romance
That was destined to take full bloom.

Where is it written,
When one is so smitten,
They must follow their mind,
And leave temptation behind?

When life brought us together
I knew it was meant forever.
We don't have to think,
We can live life on the brink.

When introduced, as if by magic wand,
You broke my life's dull bond.
Your smooth and tender touch
Made my heart beat and blood rush.

Now my prospects are new
Your love I must win it's true.
But whether I wear rags or mink
I'm going to live life to the brink.

I feel no longer alone,
Wondering how to atone.
For a life lived so lost,
Not even a shadow it cast.

To love and feel blue
Is not for either me or you.
To love and rejoice
Is more to our choice.

Picture this my dear,
Living life year after year,
Living life for the moment,
Without any care or torment.

Playing the cards that they deal,
Doing the things that are real.
You are my ace in the hole,
You will be with me when I'm old.

Living life on the brink,
Life as smooth as a skating rink.
In my hand a cool drink
On my face a sly wink.

If it doesn't work out I think
I can always go see my shrink.

Life

Strive to be at peace with your life.

But never be satisfied with your dreams.

For your life is what you see around you.

While your dreams are what is all about you.

Life's Light

Eyes that stare at life's glare
to fathom what they see
can so easily become sore.

But at the dark of night
as thoughts are gathered they are
closed and see
so clear what they had fathomed before.

Life's Lottery

His forty some years placed him in a telling role
The struggles of life were taking their toll.
Riches and gold, when young he was told,
Would make life easier as you grow old.

But success for him just seemed not to be,
Though at times he even tried the lottery.
He just seemed to fail in all his endeavors
Be it in business or in love in this world so vast
He was the one who seemed to use up life's favors
And in the hard race of life he was ending up dead last.

But as of late he had this dark plan
If he didn't make it by forty-five.
A plan that would make it certain
He wasn't a burden alive.

WILLIAM MIJO GRANICH

He prepaid his rent on his humble third story flat,
Which would take him to his birthday of forty five.
And today was the day for which he was destined.
His intentions were ever so clear and not misintended.

He entered his hovel just before the setting of night,
It wasn't quite dark enough to turn on the light
Which hung from the ceiling in a loose loop of a knot
Tied in this manner so as not to hang too low
But he thought by plan this was his last day, so what
And turned on the switch at the side of the socket.
The swaying cordlight produced shadows on the walls so bare
As they danced to and fro they softened his thoughts and cares.

His flat was just a bed in a room to which he could relate
And a second room, a kitchen with sink and hot plate.
His only luxuries were a long handle shoe horn to put on his shoes,
An old lamp in the corner that he could clap on and off as he would choose,
A three-legged stool given him by his friends down the hall,
One they would sit on when they would come to call.
And a small screen thirteen-inch TV,
Which by standards today was a necessity.

He turned on the TV for the latest news to see
Which just then was showing the latest lottery drawing
And on the three-legged stool, his lottery ticket was lying.
One number, two, and then three and then four,
Matched his ticket as though it was it they were reading.
The next was the fifth which turned out to be twenty-four,
the last was the sixth and was as if his numbers were the script.

But between four and five and then five and six,
Life seemed to stand still, but hurried the thoughts in his head,
They just came alive and so clear and clairvoyant.
They were thoughts of life's struggles and joy and contentment.
It took this scene for him to realize
Life was pure sweetness, and his craving for it so precious.
He realized he could take failure in stride
And yet in spite of this keep intact his pride.
He thanked the Lord who gave him the sight
To penetrate the dark layers of doubt.

The jackpot was seven million in gold, US currency.
He overcame the odds and a winner was he.
But his real victory was to realize his life was worth much more
And this he proved to himself beyond any score.
The winning ticket never to be cashed at all

As he burned it to ashes in a platter on the three-legged stool
Right there in his walk up third story flat
He knew he had grown up to be the man he was at last
And realized that life was, even with its struggles, for him to enjoy.
From that day he was a complete man
Whose heart was filled with joy because of the lottery
And from that day forward his life began.

Love and Joy

I've thirsted for love,
From its cup I drank.

I've felt joy,
From its soft touch
I've rejoiced.

But why are you
So special to me?

As I thirst for you,
You whisper to me,
My skin's touch
Is ever so soft,
As yours is
On me.

Lust or Love

I saw the naked body of lust
She came to me in my dreams
And said in her I must trust
If I were to fulfill my schemes
Of achieving what I have desired
When first we met and I conspired
To hold you in my arms
And fathom all your charms

I must plot and plan my actions
Carefully and without distractions
My goal must be laid out precisely
And steps taken so exactly
Because there is a real chance

That what I really want is your love

For wanting and craving and daring
Are all part of the plot
But holding and caring and sharing
Is what it is all about

The results over the span of time
Could then be mine, all mine
With my lust turned into love
As a gift from heaven above

Magical Words

For a legal pad the words were not meant.
But to freeze a memory of a heart beat spent,
Or catch a moment of happiness in one's cupped palms,
Are words that always will be their soul's balm.

Life is struggling and clawing and trying to foment
The joy to be found in words spoken in a moment.
But the memories they create are joys everlasting
And to a starved and hungry soul break its fasting.

But to whom life is joy and feelings to be cherished,
Are words that penetrate the soul and forever nourish.
As there is no sweeter love spoken or not
Than that which comes from the heart to the heart.

Mama, Do I Have to Brush my Teeth, Especially at my End?

Mama, I just had my last meal on condemned row.
Do I have to brush my teeth before I go to my end?
I've tried to remember all the things you taught me as a little boy.
I've tried to follow your words as best I could, and that the Lord truly knows.

And that lesson, the one on turning my other cheek,
I always did Mama, but the last time,
That last time was the undoing of my soul.

She said she found a better man, and Lord knows I heard that before.
I've had my share of loves and lovers, too.
But that last one, that last one was the undoing of my soul.

I asked her not to do that to me.
I'm a good man, Mama, who loved her more than any man ever could,
And that too the Lord truly knows.

Don't go out tonight I said.
Just brush your teeth and come back to me in our bed.

The last thing I can remember, Mama,
And I know it will be the last thought in my head,
The last thought I'll have, walking those final steps to my end.
If I can't have you, no man ever will.
Especially this last one, the one who won't love you like I love
You right up to the end.

The gunshot doesn't wake me or even scare me a bit.
What I'm scared of Mama, is you won't forgive me, even after my end.
So Mama, please forgive me and especially
If I don't brush my teeth before I go to meet my end.

Mature Love

My youth has slowly turned to age
My thoughts from sharp to sage.

A walk that once stepped lively
Now treads the path more lightly.

Things that have changed with the passing of time
Are all explained in living this life of mine.
But the ones that have improved with age
Are you and my love that you engage.

I used to dream of holding you so tight
I now do so with even more delight.

My days were filled with thoughts of you
Now my nights are included in this revue.
Being with you the whole day through
Makes my night holding you my dream come true.
You have completely captured my soul and heart.
You were meant for me right from the start.

I now give my love to you to hold;
Please treat it gently as we grow old.

Maturity

Crawling and walking and trotting
and then running - childhood.

Learning and reading and understanding
and then knowing - adulthood.

Longing and desiring and craving
and then having - manhood.

Looking and searching and finding
and then sharing - maturity.

My life as a babe through the
travails of childhood.

The agony of growing through lessons
of adulthood.

Knowing who you are and what
your manhood is about

Leads to understanding victory and
what in defeat is doubt.

All of my life has led to you.

All of my days now are up to you.

I can now be complete and whole,
you at my side as we grow old.

Maturity II

Crawling and walking and trotting
and then running - childhood.

Learning and reading and understanding
and then knowing - adulthood.

Longing and desiring and craving
and then having - manhood.

Looking and searching and finding

and then sharing - maturity.

My life as a babe through the
travails of childhood.

The agony of growing through lessons
of adulthood.

What have I learned through
all of these phases?
What more can I expect from
life's pages?

Knowing who I am and what my
life is about
Leads to understanding myself
without any doubts.

All of my life has led up to you
and as far as I can see I like the view.

I can now be complete, happy
and whole,
You by my side as we face
the world.

Meadow of Clover

You are a meadow of clover I
want to shortcut through
to reach my journey's end. But
I dare not as the fence that
protects you is littered with
trespass signs that I must
respect as I walk
along the road.

Longingly I look into you
and imagine a grove of Red Oak
and Sycamore. You are so inviting.
I begin to dream of what could be.
A brookling stream with soft,
pleasant banks. Inviting,

so tempting, your bubbling,
murmuring calling to me.

Come lie at my side, rest and cool your bare feet in me.
Cross me to the other side.
I am here for you, pleasure yourself,
Indulge in me.

But then I stub my toe on a boulder on the road
And imagination shifts to reality.
I am on the road alone walking beside you
and the fence that keeps us apart.
Let me reach a gate that welcomes me,
show me a sign, invite me into your meadow.
I need to rest and recharge my life on your banks.

Are you my forbidden path or dare
I scale the fence to reach you and
like the Red Oak and Sycamore and
the soft green grass on your banks
take root and build my life with you,
and enjoy the pleasures
that nature dictates for me?

More Than a Flagpole

I'm just a flagpole they say
As people pass by and look my way.

I'm proud of my heritage and past.
Solid straight maple and built to last.

When I was growing up I thought of what I wanted to be
Tucked away in the forest and nestled among all those trees.

I could have ended up as firewood and ashes
Or cut down and made into toothpicks or matches
Or a maple rocker and carried off to some lonely room
Enjoyed by only a few and have become old way too soon.

But I was proud to be carted away to be a flagpole
At a workshop with artisans forming and polishing my sides and finish
Purchased by some patriotic souls
To stand in their community day and night.
And where many look and marvel and salute my flying flag

And where would my flag fly if it were not for me?

I have a friend who stands erect in Washington D.C.
Stands among his friends and is there for the world to see
People gaze at his form as they look and see
And his like who are extruded from metal
Poured and made to size from iron and scrap metal.

While I'm in front of city hall and know my friends envy me
Standing so straight and erect and made of maple
Standing day and night always on vigil
And always pointing the way to heaven
Even when no one is looking for direction
At night I'm constantly pointing to the stars
And when it is clear I'm pointing to Venus and Jupiter and Mars.

Day or night I'm always standing there
Rain or shine, snow or sleet I'm there because I care
with my flag furling or without that is what it is all about.

People display flags on cars or trucks or trolleys
At times on the sides of buildings or anywhere they fancy.

Many are in temporary places selected by those around
Like car car tops or hood ornaments or even buildings surround.
Sometimes it's vogue to display the flag's likeness on clothes.

Little sticks carry flags while held in children's hands
Others display them on windows or are a part of marching bands.
But when the flag is hoisted up my side
That's the real McCoy and saluted with pride.
Flags get worn and others take their place to fly
But they always look to me on whom they can rely.

I've seen people from other countries look at me to visualize.
How their flag would appear on me while flying in the breeze.

And at evening time or when snow or sleet and thunder fill the sky
And I have no flag to fly
Lightning flashes reveal my
Stalwart stance which no one can deny.

And when morning dawns and a new day has begun
I'm standing there proudly to accept the flag again.
They wait for the sun to rise to unfurl the flag for the day
And at sunset I'm visited to give them back the flag I displayed.

At times children use me as a base around which to play tag.
I join them at their games all the while proudly displaying my flag.

Little ones try to hide behind my frame
to fool others while playing their game.

During special holidays when bands march and trumpets blow
I mark the start or finish for the marchers below.

At election time politicians construct their stands in my shadow
Upon which to deliver their speeches to the throngs on hand.
And when they implore the crowd to honor our nation.
It's me they stand and face as they salute or give invocation.

Some even judge the time of day by the length of my shadow
As it lies and stretches itself upon the pavement below
And because it looks so bold and strong
Little children try to jump over it as they walk along.

At times a bird will perch on the top of me
Small children notice this and are quick to see
The bird was headed in a direction the other way
But decided to rest and catch his breath and for awhile decided to stay

There's always this personal feeling when someone leans on me
Or when lunches are taken at my base at noon or high tea.
Meet you at the flagpole is a common directional phrase
Because I'm always here and they can plan on this place.

I've outlasted wars and storms and various administrations.
I've witnessed children and adults of many generations.
I've even had those who try to shimmy up me
But end up at my base with sore knees.

With a twist of fate I could have been a tadpole
But as heaven would have it I ended up a flagpole.

My personal calling is right here in this square for all to see
I am a part of this nation and am proud so to be.

My Calendar

My calendar hanging on the wall consists of just one day
Hanging on the wall of my life in full display
And I need not turn the page from day to day
As every today is like every tomorrow
It marks the day we met and as I looked into your eyes
I knew at that moment I did not want the day to pass
Or to look ahead to tomorrow because I wanted today to last
The hours of my day are measured by your charms revealed
The minutes are my sighs of love unsealed
And each ticking moment of my heart murmurs
The constant beat of I love you, I love you, I love you.

My Creation of You

My thirsting longing for love is my incentive
To pray to heaven above and be inventive
My thoughts become words of reality
Creating you is then mere formality.

Words become visions to describe you
Creating a form that becomes so true
A form that takes shape before my eyes
As your radiant glow reveals your many charms.

Among all of your charms are your two luscious lips
That I just can't find the strength to resist.
And when I look into your eyes
I am completely mesmerized.
When I think how your heart is about to throb
Mine is about to stop.
When I dream of you
I want my creation to come true.

Now my dilemma is compounded.
My mind, my thoughts are impounded.
What am I to do
With this creation that is you?

Am I destined to search this would so vast
Until I find you at long last
Or did I create you for my dreams in a world unreal
Where we can be lovers forever and ever
As my love for you I reveal?

WILLIAM MIJO GRANICH

My Furry Little Friend

I saw this squirrel that left its tree
To me it appeared to be walking around aimlessly
But with a little more scrutiny
I concluded foraging for food was a more certainty.

He didn't have a supermarket to shop,
Or a place for his credit card to plop.
I could see he didn't have a pocket for his change,
Or visible signs of barter he could arrange.

As he looked at me he seemed to say:
"What can you do for me for heaven's sake?"
Now as an adult I have all the benefits of barter
And ways and means to obtain my larder.

A few crackers I had in my pantry
So I tossed them at his feet just outside my entry.
Closed my screen door and went inside my house
To write this poem about the rodent that was not a mouse.

In a while I heard this noise at the door
And I'll be if those crackers he didn't devour.
The scratching on my screen was his way of asking for more.
This time I made sure he had plenty to keep him occupied
And even some to hide in his secret domicile.

Now I have a new furry little friend that lives in that tree,
The tree that I now know is his house.
A furry little rodent that is not a mouse,
Who always seems to smile at me.

My furry little friend with the bushy tail
Who thinks he has me figured in great detail.
And he could be right, or not,
But who cares, I just know he pleases me a lot.

And when he sees me each day anew,
He greets me with a smile and good cheer,
And in his own way seems to say,
"Greetings my friend, the top of the mornin' to you!"

POEMS AND PROSE

My Holidays

It is not important for us on any one day to be together.
What is important is we found each other for now and forever.

You were in my thoughts before I met you.
You were in my dreams before I even knew.
You are the one that kept me single,
You are the one that makes my heart tingle.

Holidays are days of joy
Meant for all to enjoy.
Commemorating special occasions
With food and drink and decorations.

But the days that are cause for my celebrations
And this I decided after great deliberation,
Is the first day I met you in all your grace,
And all the days that have followed since.

My Journey

I have traveled the countryside,
At times even circled the globe.
Some journeys have been simple,
Others turned out to be bold.

I've used sextant and compass and maps,
Itineraries laid out in detail and exact.
Some trails took dead reckoning,
Others followed the beaten path.

Each road has a beginning and end.
Each trail a start and many bends.
A highway is marked by signs and directions,
A river flows to its end without interruption.

But the one path I seem always to choose,
The one path that needs no markings,
The path for which I'm always longing
Is the path that leads directly to you.

WILLIAM MIJO GRANICH

My Life is On Hold

I can't believe I am living this life.
Who would believe all of my strife?
Another week will pass so blue,
Another week without a call from you.

Not even a hint of happiness for me.
Nary a crumb of compassion can I see.
If my life were played by the rules
The outcome would not be so cruel.

Three strikes and you be out,
The worst is back to the dug out.
Ball four and you walk
At least on the bases I can talk.

A missed basket is not so bad,
I'd not be a bent and broken lad.
A gutter ball I could bowl,
At least in my heart there would be no hole.

But striking out with you on my mind
Is shooting an airball in full view of mankind.
Waiting to hear the telephone ring,
Hoping the next call will be the real thing.

Maybe when all this torture is done
I can shake the blues and have some fun.

This waiting by the telephone is sad,
Waiting to hear from you is not bad.
But not hearing from you for so long
Puts my life on hold and that is wrong.

My Lonely Love

Am I so desperate to be loved?
Am I that desperate to share my heart?
An unreturned love is not the norm,
Even a baby is loved before it is born.

A love to flourish must have a path
To travel between two hearts without wrath.
Kindness and tenderness are not things we learn,

They are traits inherent in our hearts as we yearn.

To give love to the ones we cherish
So that in return our hearts will not perish.
But a love dampened by tears of loneliness
Is a lonely love doomed to suffer in a world of hopelessness.

So close your eyes and see my prayers,
Open your heart and hear my pleas.
Embrace me with your arms and when it's done,
We'll hold on so tight our hearts become one.

My Love

My love is zeroed on you as its target.
It is directed at you with complete precision.
You are the object of its flight,
And when it touches you with its warmth
And you respond in like kind to me
then for the moments eternal so be it.

We become one in unison during its eternal flight.
For you are the megaphone of my love.
You amplify my love as it envelopes all there is to be.
All objects, all life, all thought now and to be.
I love you and everyone and everything for I love me.

My Misty Image

The fretwork of my mind
Appears through stained glass windows
Differentiating the naked form
Of a body so milky white and warm.

It sharpens my eye and warms this heart of mine.
The foggy mist settles on the surface of my mind
As I wipe it away with a concerted sigh
And a brisk, delicate brush of imagination.

Who is this image for whom I long?
Her heart I know, my devotion just grows,
Her face needs more focus in my mind.
Please unveil, please undress this décolletage.

My mind I assail, my heart must prevail.
I plead, I long, I crave, I am tantalized
I will give completely of me, all of me
Give me a sign so that I will believe in what I visualize.

My Oasis

You are my oasis of desire, my lover.
And I a parched and wanting traveler
Thirst for your drops of love as they overflow
To quench my thirst of longing and wanting.
My hand cupped and eagerly awaiting
To catch drop by drop the food for my soul.
I raise my hand to my face
So careful not to spill any drop of love
And as I await the next moist pearl of love's overflow,
Lick the last droplet of love's sweet nectar
From my trembling hand
As though from my soul.

My Path

A good coat makes a cold man warm.
A fawn is hungry the moment it is born.
Money makes a miser feel rich,
A steady hand keeps a car out of the ditch.

Riches and clothes and food and drink
Satisfy many needs as quick as a wink.
But what I seem to crave and desire
Is a friend with whom I can conspire
To make the cold days turn warm
And the happy days seem the norm.

Like Diogenes with lantern searching for a man of truth
My heart reaches out to find the route.
Through the world's maze of paths
To a love that can only last,
Whose deeds are kind and to me reveal
That the path I'm on is truly real.

My Prescription for Me

I get advice from varied sources about my well being.
Much of it concerns my heart and tips for long living.
My doctor talks of cholesterol,
It must be controlled above all.

The therapist says relax you must,
Heed my advice or you'll end up as dust.

My trainer tells me, keep moving and exercise,
For if you do not it is not too wise.

The dietician recommends calories keep low,
Or they might be lowering you in a box below.

Even my financial advisor gives advice,
Follow it and you need not think twice.

I listen to all these sage instructions
And follow them to prevent my destruction.

But what they don't understand or see
That when it comes to what's best for me.

In spite of all the advice they give about my heart,
And they all mean well right from the start.

You control my heart and control its beat
You are the one who makes it tick and at times skip a beat.

So cholesterol, calories,
Exercise, sage advice, or what
Wrap them all in a prescription
And tie them with a knot.

The best prescription I have for me
And that to me is plain to see
Is to take a dose of you the whole day through
And one at night to make my dreams come true.

WILLIAM MIJO GRANICH

My River

I love it when you can't say I love you.
But I'd love it even more if you'd try.
I love it when you scold me for being me.
But I'd love it even more if it needn't be.

I try to earn your love in every way.
I only wish I didn't have to try today.
I loved you before we met.
You know my love is here to stay.

True love is undying like an ancient river.
But it must be fed by nature's snows.
My river runs within my soul,
Fed by teardrops of love and joy.

My river is filling for all to see.
So chart the course where it can flow,
Sandbag the banks for the overflow.
Come ride my river to our destiny.

My Secret Dream

You are my secret dream.

When my days have their say,
And my nights turns into dreams,
You slide down moon beams
And tumble into my arms.

I don't dare reveal to anyone
What pleasure we find in us,
As we frolick the night away,
For then you woullldn't be my secret dream.

Like the shadows that move at dusk
To fill the valleys below,
My love for you fills
The valleys of my heart.

And when the new dawn unfolds,
I secret you in my heart,
That beats for you with all its might

As I await the moonbeams
Of another night.

My Soul's Flight

My soul wanders through the chambers of my heart
And casts shadows on my heart's walls
All the while waiting to do my bidding.

Time will take time for my soul to know
You are my object of life and delight
The one who can launch my soul into full flight.

As it seeks to follow your soul's journey
So that our two souls can embrace in eternity
And we not wonder if there is a there
For then we will know that everywhere is there.

My Temptation, My Obsession

When I look at you with all your allure
I just breathe a sigh and know for sure
You are a dangerous, magnificent temptation,
A pure tantalizing thrill, my obsession.

My wildest thoughts swirl around your body
As my inhibitions pay attention to nobody.
But my emotions I must always control
Or in your army of suitors I would enroll
And march to the tune of your beat.
But with your legions I cannot compete.

How best can I describe your captivating charms
And stay within society's accepted bounds?
You are a tempest in an angel's body and mind.
I surrender my resistance, so please be kind.

WILLIAM MIJO GRANICH

Names

I've always wondered what's in a name
And can that alone bring fame?

Did Sir Lancelot ride his horse a lot?
Or was King Arthur the people's greatest benefactor?
And then I wonder a lot
Why did they both live in Camelot?

Did the Count of Monte Cristo
Ever visit San Francisco?
Or did he learn to cook with Crisco
So when all was done he would disco?

Do famous people end up with famous names?
Are ordinary ladies just ordinary dames?
And why is the common guy perceived as without a tie?

But it is not the name that makes one famous.
It is the deeds that keep him from being nameless.
So my advice to you is fill your life with deeds.
Only then can you be famous and achieve your needs.

Be you Sir Lancelot or king Arthur or what's his name,
Thump your chest, trumpet your horn and be
        proud of your name.

Nothing, Something, Everything

Once not so long ago
She met this man and asked
So many questions
they caught his attention.

What do you do – his reply, nothing.
Where do you go – nowhere.
What do you want – nothing.
Who do you need – no one.

his answers though puzzling, he felt were true to him,
For he was happy within.
But his answers were hollow,
There was no path his heart could follow.

Then in due time they embraced,
A spark was lit.
His heart was touched a bit.
He felt his life was changing its pace.

What do you want to do – something.
Where do you want to go – somewhere.
What do you want – something.
Who do you need – someone, maybe you.

Soon love came to full bloom,
His heart found all kinds of room
To do, to want, to aspire and dream,
For life held prospects of peaches and cream.

What do you do – everything.
Where do you go – everywhere.
What do you want – everything.
Who do you need – you and everyone.

But especially you, my love.
As you showed my heart the path it should follow
To a life in which dreams can come true
And my life no longer lies fallow.

Nurtured Flower

Oh my beautiful long stemmed American Beauty.
You make me think how life could be.
You are a flower that has taken root in my heart,
A flower nurtured by my tears when we are apart.
If we were together the sun would always shine
And glow in my heart as I would know you are mine.

There is so much to be said,
So many thoughts run through my head.
So much feeling in my heart,
Words are not enough when we are apart.

I need to feel your presence,
Hold you close and hold you tightly,
Know that in all of life's lessons
Yours is a love I cannot take lightly.

WILLIAM MIJO GRANICH

So dream of me as I dream of you,
And pray for us so that we may be
Two nurtured flowers in life's garden of love,
With the radiant sun shining on us from above.

One Day At A Time

Today was an easy day for me.
Just one box of tissues to dry away my tears.
Just one box in composing my plea.
Be gentle, be kind and sweep away my fears.

Today I can listen to my heart that I can now trust.
For my tears have washed away all of its doubts.

And like the miner who staked his claim of old
And spent his life panning the river in search of his vein of gold.
I can spend my life plucking the chords of my heart that touch my very soul
To compose the symphonic masterpiece whose melody will make me whole.

And if I think today is a waste of time
There is always tomorrow that will be all mine.
To shed a few more tears and feel more sorrow
To cleanse not only my heart but also my soul of desire.

Our Campsite at Lake Siskiyou

Is that God peeking out behind
Mt. Shasta, the snow laden slopes
looking like his beard?

The slender pines racing toward the
sky, each striving to be the first
to brush the underside of heaven.

A wise and smug mirror lake
reflecting the snowy mountains.
Tolerating the swimmers and
pleasure crafts seeming to know
it was here before mankind and

confident it will endure all
their trespasses.

And we just two of God's
subjects drinking in, chewing and
tasting the pleasure of the sky,
the mountains, the majestic lake
and forest with its shoreline and
our borrowed campsite.

Borrowed because it is God's real property
and we just two fleeting tenants.

Our Fantastic Flights

In day my thoughts seemed so pure,
But in my subconscious I was not so sure.

In sleep I could frolick through the night,
And do as I might.
The devil I need not pay.
Im fact I'd do as I may.
The devil could take the hindmost,
No rules to follow, no signposts.

I could be cunning in my thoughts,
Devious in my plots.
I could err in my judgment,
Not be punished by self denouncement.

But many are the times I'd wake at night,
Shaking and trembling and startled with fright.
I didn't know what to believe,
In sight I could see no relief.

It seemed so incredible,
My thoughts so indelible,
Etched as false treasures
In my dream time of pleasures.

My day thoughts and night dreams were far apart.
Ones were of me, in the others I
could just revel
In this pact made with the devil.

My intentions were out of control.
How could I mend?
Or was it to be so to the end?
Must I so suffer,
And have no hope to recover?

But then I met you,
And all this was oh so untrue
I pulled you into my dreams.
You became my lightning rod for love.
Now my thoughts are as from
Heaven above.

Now I can look into my thoughts
And feel it in my heart,
That you are the one,
As my heart you have won.

You are the object of my delight.
You launch my fantasies every flight
Into an orbit of the moon.
An orbit that developed real soon
Into a world of heart felt things.

In a life full of kisses and hugs,
In both the days and nights,
As we journey on our fantasy's flights.

Our Lake of Love

My life was as calm as a lonely mountain lake.
No confusions, no illusions, just give as much as you take.
The breezes would dance through my tranquil world,
And at times I would join them in their mystical swirl.

The only ripples I felt were from life's occasional rain.
Tiny little ripples that in time would refrain.

Then along came you, a beautiful bird in full flight,
And splashed in my world and caused my plight.

Your impact on me made ripples to dissipate to the shore.
But to my amazement I found I wanted more.

My calm became excited as you bathed to my touch,
And I felt my life changing just experiencing such.

Wanting you to stay to make my life calm again.
Wishing you would improve my life in the bargain.
Wanting more of you, more of your charm.
Thrilling me and exciting me but I knew what you did to my calm,
And I also knew as you rested from your flight,
When you entered my world everything would be right.

The calm that you now create in my life everyday
Is the return of my love for which I did pray.
And now as I look back across our tranquil lake,
I have the gift of our love which I will never forsake.

Our Love

Our lives have changed as youth has blossomed to age.
Our thinking is clear but is now even more sage.
Though we've known each other just a short while,
Especially as measured by life's turnstile
Of hopes and dreams and problems to solve,
I know now that together as a couple is our resolve.

Last night's encounter was tender and pure mature love.
And we can thank for this the powers above
In repaying us for lost years by the sprinkling of stardust last night
That circled our bodies and lives to make us together everything right.
Two fortunate people reaping the prize of love's lottery
And meant to recapture the life of before we met
To enjoy what we now have as our kismet

We now know we must live in the present
And savor the joys with no resentment.
As we proved last night with our bodies and limbs entwined
Not knowing what part was yours and what was mine.
Frolicking around like two bear cubs in a heap
Wondering if what would be left of us was enough to keep,
We can now approach life with calm and resolute
Our feelings so deep, so pure and absolute.

Our life is a kaleidoscope of love realized in reams
For we now share our lives and dreams.
Who would have thought that in our future

WILLIAM MIJO GRANICH

We could look back over the years
And see our life together with our share of laughs and tears,
Now tears of joy and happiness, oh, so deep.
The combinations of numbers in love's lottery are endless.
Winning love's lottery was fate and now is ours to keep.

Our Own World of Two

I know no one who is world renowned
Or one whom they must gather around,
One who has caused a thousand sabres to rattle,
Or led other brave men into battle.

But in our world measured by my love,
Whose boundaries are defined by your needs,
And the whole world is just you and me,
I feel I am more than all of the above.

My heart has been captured by your beauty.
My soul has surrendered itself to you completely.
My thoughts are only of what you need.
My lust is commanded by your deeds.

To make our world of two complete,
We must fulfill our dreams as we repeat
Those vows on our world's most important day.

The day that we celebrate each other anew
And in our hearts and souls we both knew
It was true love when we both said I do.

Passion, Jealousy, and Hate

In the song they sing of passion, jealousy and hate
That makes it very difficult for me to relate.

In my heart for you I have passion,
For you and only you are the one I fashion.

I feel jealous when you are not in my arms,
But it is only because I am jealous for your charms.

But for them to sing of hate,
I feel that is just a waste.
I think of you as holding the key
    to my heart's gate.
For you and you alone are my
    passion, jealousy and fate.

Please Be Real

I close my eyes and see you so clearly.
I am in a state of swirling warm feelings.
The light reflects off your soft curvaceous form.
Are you my imagination or are you flesh?
Are you my wish, my wants, my desires, my all?
Can I approach you, do I dare?

What is your name, who are you?
What may I call you? Please be real.
Do you know how much I care?
Are you the answer to my prayers?

You are so close, may I reach out and touch you?
Don't vanish from me, my life you will be.
Can we connect, can we embrace and hold?
Can we plan and dream, can we be real?

You are inerasably etched in my heart's wants.
My reckless, foolish thoughts
Replaced by pure, warm feelings.
You are my secret longings
Exposed in a confession of love.
Shall I wait for you? Please wait for me.
I know you will be real
As our souls are now in an everlasting embrace.

Primer for Life

Life is a huge teeter totter.
We and the world and all its problems are on one end.
The fulcrum placed exactly in the middle is reality.
The balance is made possible by our hopes and dreams.
And wherever in the world that equilibrium becomes more than a dream

WILLIAM MIJO GRANICH

Peace and joy and happiness will everlastingly reign supreme.

Pure Pleasure and Joy

There are not many pure pleasures
      a man has in life.
But beholding your beautiful breasts is one of
      the pure pleasures in my life.

It thrills me beyond explanation
      and excites my senses beyond real reason.

In my dreams I brush
      my imagination over your beautiful breasts
      and breathe pure joy into my life.

Just as two butterflies brush and kiss a beautiful flower
    in life's garden of love and bring beauty
    and joy into this world for all to see.

And when my day turns into sleep
    my heart cries out in sad lore.
Please come to me in my dreams tonight
    so my heart is not sad
    and will weep no more.

Reaching for the Stars
or
Communication On a Dark Corner During Super Bowl Week in Miami

Stick 'em up!
Stick what up?
Your arms, Mac!
Oh, is this a hold up?
It ain't no touchdown, Jack.

REALITY

I'm not fooled that the stork standing there has only one leg.
Or that freshly shorn sheep in the distance is only shorn on this side.
Or that water runs uphill as I'm standing on my head.
And I'm not fooled by your charms as I hold you in my arms.

Because I've seen that stork as it was about to fly.
And I've seen that sheep up close to me from both sides.
And standing on my head things just get turned upside down.

But what you can prove of your charms
That I have always felt with you in my arms
Is to fill my long lasting fantasy
And whisper to me that you are my destiny.

Redemption

To be happy I need to claim my redemption
For all the pleasures in life I went without.
It need not be a huge revelation
But enough to cure my happiness drought.

I was not born into royalty
Nor with silver spoon in mouth.
I have not achieved immortality
Nor nearly accomplished what I set about.

I see no magic solution in sight
But know what is wrong from right.
You are the one that holds the key
the one to turn the latch and set me free.

You are the one who has my devotion
The one who has allowed me to dream again
And made me whole and happy in the bargain.
Sharing life with you would be my redemption.

Relationships

A relationship is like a pair of shoes.
You first see them in a storefront
window and the clerk presents
them in their best light,
patently shiny and glistening in their uniqueness.
then you take them home and
as you first wear them they seem a little stiff and even a
bit uncomfortable. But as

time goes by they shape and
mold and stretch and fold and
are a genuine comfort – so much
like they were meant to be,
and then all too soon they seem
worn and you are faced with
the thoughts of discarding them
and shopping for replacements.
But my love let us not fall
into that trap, that cycle of life.
Let you and I forever go barefoot
over the meadows and trails
of life. Let us prance and
dance through our daily lives.
We do not need the emotional
confinements on our lives.
I have you and you have me.
Let us rejoice barefoot in the park
for all the world to see.

Rewards

Do you seek bounty for each heart conquered?
Or a medal for the deeds you perform?
Do you crave applause for each brilliant moment?
Or rapture from the words you've spoken?

Do you weigh the rewards of your actions
Or exalt in the din of applause?

If so, your character is thin my friend,
Like the shallow puddle after the rain,
Stagnant and ready to dry up in vain.

It is the thinness of a shadow
Cast by the stature of a real being
You need the sun to shine
To claim you are among the living.

And if the sun does not shine,
You are not there, you are nowhere.

So be whole in your endeavors
And modest in your achievements.
The world will recognize and reward

All the good you bring forward.

And happiness and joy
Will be your bounty to enjoy.

Save For a Rainy Day

My papa always told me and othesr around me told me too,
Put away and save for a rainy day, and that's what I would do.

Save and put away those pieces of silver and coins of gold,
For you'll need them, and that's for sure as you grow old.

But there were other things worth saving that no one told me about.
Things I had to figure out all by myself and learn without a doubt.

Things I would lock away and keep in my vault just for that rainy day.
And most of these were things I learned from loving you, I would have to say.

Good thoughts and good feelings and memories we would share.
Laughs and joys and giggles as we each received as much as we gave.

Days and nights of happiness also wrapped up in the love we shared,
And all the while not knowing we were putting away memories because we cared.

Then there comes the time we all must dig deep into ourselves,
And reach for those memories that are put away and ours to do as we may

And having those memories is so precious to us now.
For we loved each other then just as much as we love each other now.

Schemes or Dreams

Do I dare dream?
Or do I resort to scheme?
Dreams are just thoughts,
Schemes are real plots.

Do I you bed
On the chance we would wed?
Or do I just scheme
With you in my dreams?

In a dream I am serene
In a plot I am not,
You were sent to me from above,
I want you to be my love.

I've thought of this a lot,
A scoundrel I am not.
So in conclusion
This is my solution.

To make you part of my schemes
Would make life not worth a dime.
I'll keep you in my dreams
For then you are mine, and only mine.

Scorpio Man, Aries Woman

Scorpio man deals with love as a known,
I deal with the feelings I've always known.
When Aries woman came into my life,
I felt the world was not all contrite.

The words and the thoughts we shared
Were at times meant as a dare.
You seemed receptive and daring
Did I mistake this for caring?

I know my words were not always chosen
With careful thought and perception.
I opened the door of my past
Because I felt our love could last.

I opened the door to the future
For I thought of myself as your tutor.
But when in your step you did hesitate
And instead fell back to meditate,
I felt the lack of forward movement
Was certainly not an improvement.

Did my words seem so deep
Or did they startle you like a fawn from its sleep?
Did my measure of life
Give you reason to believe

I was thinking of a wife?
Or did you think to discover
I was seeking a lover?

Let me quickly dispense any fear or doubt
your love means more to me than what I'm about.

Now I'm holding the door open to our future,
The world is ours to nurture.
Our lives are at the center of the universe,
Our love for each other is not in reverse.

Are our lives written in the stars of Astrology?
Or do we need to fall back on plain old Anthropology?
Scorpio man, Aries woman, do yourselves
    proud and meld into one.
Let the world see what we've begun.

I'm standing here my soul naked in fear.
Step over the threshold and embrace me my dear.
For only then will our hearts feel glee,
And only then will our love be free.

Searching For Love

Hi diddle diddle
Life is just a riddle
One of the problems to solve
Is where to find love.

I think I am whole and completely free.
But then love plays a trick on me.
My actions are calculated to be just mine,
But each movement is made with love in mind.

I plan my days to enjoy
But truly I'm just love's toy.
It's not that I don't savor this role,
I only wish that love I could control.

I wake in the morning with great intent
By noon I'm lonely and longing for love's content.
All day I perform my chores with resolve,
All the while my thoughts are where to find love.

And when night descends to end the day,
I'm the first in line for love to pray.
Dear Lord please set me free,
Help me find my love for me.

Searching for Love 2

As I lay down and try to sleep,
My love is yours alone to keep.

My passion for you runs so deep,
When it is unleashed I feel I cannot sleep.

Last night my love for you was evident,
My feelings spilled from my heart in contentment.

Last night my tears that brushed on your cheek
Were not of a man that is weak or meek.

They were tears of passion and joy,
Tears of love not meant to destroy.

As I lay my head on my pillow,
My body feels like a swaying willow.

I try to be still and lonely on my bed,
Thoughts of love roll around in my head.

Endless thoughts run through my mind,
Thoughts I must analyze one at a time.
But the uppermost thought in my mind,
Is your true love that I somehow must find.

Six Phases of Love

There are six phases leading to love I'm told.
And each is a phase unto itself and old as the world is old.

It doesn't matter where you perform them or whether or not
It could be here or there or anywhere
as what matters are the thoughts.

But you must know the rules of love and respect

And believe in all the phases with circumspect.

The first phase is the meeting or the hugging and I know
We all need this phase for us to grow.
Hugging the person you are holding
And let them feel they are the one you are wanting.
Just hold tight and gently squeeze to true delight.
And always give as much as you receive or got.

The second phase is the daring or the one of kissing.
This phase is always a clear indication
Of what you are missing or know that you are in
for an education.

The lips can be kissed or the cheeks or the eyes
The lobes of the ears, the chest or even the thighs.

You can select your lips' target and
deliver the feelings so right.
the gently pressed pressure of warm
throbbing anticipation.
Open lips, closed lips slowly or
in wild syncopation.
Don't hurry or hold back any portion
of your desires of delight.

And remember the trails of sensations
your lips are creating
And know that you can always retrace the
warm path of craving.

The third phase is the wanting or the back rub
and must not be taken lightly.
It's always available and conveniently at the ready.

No special places are needed for
its implementation
No judge of performance is expected
of its execution.

This can be performed on a couch
or in a crowded room
In an elevator or park or
dancing to your favorite tune.

The back is your field of play from the
neck to the waist.

Linger awhile, stroke softly, move slowly
and never in haste.
Feel the flesh flow and coax the skin lightly
take your time and build the crescendo
to a symphony so mighty.
Light and soft, warm and hot.
strokes made smoothly
you be the judge of its effect as you feel
the returning warm breeze of anticipation.

We now come to the fourth phase, that of exploring or massage
And oh what a master of ecstasy it
is truly your message of love.

It is not merely a rub of the body
or of stroking direct
It is a language of touch and the flow of love
Between two souls who are about to connect.
your caress speaks through your hands
And your heart and is so real
Speaks volumes as you scale the
ecstasy you cannot conceal.

And as you touch and ply the
warm soft flesh for what
you dare to expect
The response is returned through
your body to your heart direct
And forms a channel from your heart
to that of the one you caress.

Let the warmth glow, let your thoughts flow.
You are both in the same world of love and content.
For this is the phase that prepares you
for the ecstasy that is about to unfold.

We are now ready for the two final stages of love.
Both are culminations of
arriving at journey's end.
these two stages of emotions
are alike as the two sides
of a coin and are no
mystery to each other.

They are not heads or tails,
win or lose, or a part of a plot.
The phases are nearly the same

but the differences a lot.
they are preceded by words of
understanding and promises to be
broken or kept.
Emotions concealed or out in full view
Feelings expressed and believed
or not so true.
So the journey's end is up to the both of you.

One is the feeling of lust and
understanding the emotions shared.
the other is the flow of truth and
believing the loves pledged.

These are phases five and six and
frankly mixed up more than not.
But either phase leads to the path of bliss
And the rewards promised by that first kiss.
Contentment and excitement and ecstasy at its best.
So hang on, goodnight, it's Christmas
and the Fourth of July, hang on tight
It's whatever holiday comes to mind
so don't delay,
Easter of Halloween, your birthday
or Lincoln's or whatever you say.

The promises made must be kept tomorrow or today
your happiness is at stake and worn as a badge
On your chest or your vest or as a corsage
It will show in your eyes and be a part of yourself.

For you now have the phases of love at your demand.
And can be practiced from phase one to six as you command.
Life is beckoning for you to put them to the test.
Use your knowledge wisely and it is
up to you to do the rest.

So, Go Figure

I can hear an ant think
Hurry, hurry, work work work work.

I know what a bee is thinking
Don't touch me and I won't sting thee.

A spider is easy to understand
While weaving his web strand after strand
Look out for the big guys
They're cleaning house, look out on all sides.

A fly as it darts from window pane to sill to wall
Says how do I get out of here and that's not all
I got to beat their swat
Those people don't appreciate me a lot.

The bird as it looks at me gliding overhead on high
Is thinking, boy I'm glad they can't fly.

And the fish as it swims in the stream
Looks over at me and knows
There is no reason to scream
Just stay calm and take care of its minnows.

I can even figure out some people.
For example some of your friends
They're wondering if we're congenial
And if not when is it about to end.

And what I ponder and also can figure
That you with your talents and charms
Look at me and in my heart trigger
The impulse to take and hold you in my arms.

For it is not only our two bodies that embrace.
It's our hearts that meld and create a place
For our love to be sparked and brought to full glow
Holding hands and walking through crowds
For all the world to know.

Society's Rules

We played the game by society's rules
Tell me now if we won or lost.
As I think back as I so often do,
Of those last moments of joy and pain
Both of us committed to social rules.

Our bodies pressed so tight as just one
Our loves warmed and melted and

flowing in each other's veins.

We both knew like travelers on opposite platforms,
Your tracks would take you one way, away from me,
My path headed the other way, and total disarray.

And yet we knew as we disembraced
This was truly the beginning of the end.
The final chapter of hoping and longing
The last page of two lives left wanting.

Storefront Faces and Hearts Not True

I walk through life
And turn the pages of time
Looking at storefront faces
And hearts that are not true.

I thought I knew you
I know I loved you
And even thought
You loved me, too.

but I could not relate
to a storefront face
With a heart not true.

I traveled life looking for love.
I searched the world
Looking for you.

But all I found
Was a storefront face
And a heart not true,
A mannequin disguised as you.

I looked into a mirror
And even looked into my heart,
And what I saw was a storefront face
And a heart so blue,
Just to survive it had to be untrue.

So now I joined the world
Of small talk and destitute.

A world of storefront faces
And hearts that are not always true.

Whose lonely nights are filled
With tears and sorrow,
thinking what the world will bring
And afraid to face tomorrow.

Tears as Big as Cookies

Your harsh words touch my heart and freeze my soul.
And when not spoken with love
It's a cloudburst from above.

Tears as big as cookies just fall and fall,
Enough to start a Girl Scout sale,
Enough to start a waterfall.

But like the sun that halts the rain
Your kind words make the sun shine again.
Shine in my heart and mind,
Shine enough to warm my very soul.

Temple of Love

Your body is the temple for my love.
Your sweet voice through word or song,
The chiming bells calling me to pay homage to my desires.
Your legs are that path my soul desires,
Your knees and thighs the stairs I require.

Your lap is that desired pew
I choose to kneel and pay my due.
I raise my head, moonlight gleaming through your auburn hair.
Fill my eyes and heart with that aura of desire.
From your shoulders to your waist
The cathedral of promise and passion
Fill my heart with deep compassion.

Your spirit is the doctrine my soul answers,
your mind the bible my heart must decipher.
My prayers are answered with complete and sweet desire.

Your body is the temple my soul requires.

Thanks for Giving

I thank you for you this Thanksgiving.
Thank you for the joy of giving.
This Thanksgiving I spent
In solitude so I could repent.

I'm sorry we never met before.
For me I never knew what was in store.
I know now the joy of receiving,
My denial of this was deceiving.

You give of yourself to everyone.
I know they all cherish you as a friend.
But I'm sorry I must insist to the end
You hold back some of yourself for this one.

Though this year Thanksgiving was traditional,
The one next year will be more special.
My hope is for both of us to give and receive
From each other the love, nurture and
        closeness only we can conceive.

The Alteration of My Life

When first we met
I never thought I'd be smitten.
Was it fate, kismet
Or in heaven so written,
In the chapters of my destiny
In the book of my life?

My life took on a progression,
Altering its path in a new direction.
And as the clouds of time rolled by
My longings were clear as the bright blue sky.

Before there were thoughts in my head
Like covet and thirst, relish and cherish.

Thoughts like desire and conspire,
Choice and rejoice.
But who knew how to put them in the proper order?
Certainly not I, for my life was in total disorder.
Now my life is clear and without pain.
My search for you was not in vain.

I knew to fill my needs,
To make me happy indeed,
To fill my void of craving
With a life full of caring,
You were the one, my passion.
With you my life I could fashion
Into one with dreams come true,
With the love I found in you.

The Balloons Will Soar No More

Oh, how the guests did celebrate.
They came to hear your sacred vows.
How each of you would dedicate
Your lives to your union so new.

The ballroom was colorful and bright.
The balloons were tugging on their ribbons so tight
To keep them from soaring into full flight.
The setting was one of complete delight.

The confetti was sparkling while floating in the air,
Twirling and dancing, reluctant to settle on tables and chairs.
Some was sprinkled in the guests' hair,
While more was atop their shoulders bare.

You and the groom were generous with yourselves,
Dancing with the guests as they were enjoying themselves.
Revelry was everywhere and merriment filled the air.
The scene could have been out of Dickens, to compare.

When the wedding party moved on
And the celebration was done
The next day was time to clear away
The festivity's doings, the party's residue.

As a friend of both you and the groom

I was a volunteer to help clean the room.
Entering the scene was like my past made no sense,
Like my future had come to an abrupt end.

The balloons now limp rolled in the draft
On tables and chairs and near the door.
Their ribbons draped and tangled around them on the floor,
No need their use, as the balloons would soar no more.

The confetti was like tears in the scene
Matching but not as plentiful as the tears in my heart.
And like the limp balloons my spirit would soar no more
The party is over and so are my dreams forever more.

When the vows were said and the sermon read
It was as though my future vanished into the air.

The guests did not know, were not aware.
No one knew, not even the groom
That you and I in days gone by
Danced in this very room.

When our hopes were high and we closed our eyes
And together we dared to dream for more.
But now our sighs and hopes
Have turned into promises unkept.

What went astray, what caused our plan's betrayal?
It seemed it was just awhile I was away.
Your letter tried to explain it so clearly that day
But now as I think through my clouded tears
I can't remember the reasons you gave.

I'll never forget that little kiss, just a peck
You courteously bestowed on me.
The guests were watching, the party was in full swing
And my gallantry, though confused, was held in check.

Just as when the vows were said and that part was read
"Speak now or forever hold your peace,"
Was the sealing of my fate, something I will always dread,
The beginning of when my dreams would cease.

Now I must vanish into exile, relegate
All my sorrows and heartaches

All my dreams of love, my plans for joy
And mask my feelings, keep away from the world
The hurt that has been done
The aching that has begun.

I'm left with the last meager memory of you
That last peck of a kiss, our fond adieu.

The glasses empty or with traces of wine or champagne
Will be cleaned and washed and neatly stored away.
But my hopes and dreams are now my closed chapter of lore.

The balloons and ribbons and confetti will be gathered
Thrown into the trash and carted away
Just as my hopes and dreams are shattered
And must be forgotten and not live another day.

But the tears in my heart will always stay
As they are all I have left from us,
For the rest of my days
For the rest of my life
Until I am dust.

The Beginning of Love

A wise man once said
One should decide with their head,
Decisions from the heart
Are not always smart.

I know you have loved before.
Was your heart hurt to the core?
Or was it broken
By harsh words that were spoken?

But why is it now so hard
To say for all to hear,
I love you, I love you,
I truly do my dear?

Let's analyze that little phrase,
Examine each word, one at a time,
When whispered softly together,

Would make you mine forever.

Is it the word I
That when said
Comes from your head
Instead of through a sigh?

Is it the admission of love
You feel must be so strong
That to say it and not mean it
You feel is so wrong?

Or is it the you
When uttered out loud,
Must be so true
It's like parting of the clouds?

Though I have never loved before
I can say I love you.
I will love you until I die,
And I say this without a lie.

So my love, say it in your heart.
For that at least is the start.
It need not be verbalized,
But in your heart it will be analyzed.

And if there comes a time
When like a poem our lives do rhyme
That will mark the beginning of love,
The beginning of you and me.

The Bird That Didn't Sing

When into the woods goes little Mille
So sweet is her song.

All the birds gather around
Gather around little Millie.

Then all the birds from all of the trees
Fly to the sea, fly far to the sea.

Only one remains behind
The one who could not sing.

Poor little birdie,
She stays behind to keep company with little Millie.

The Call

You said you would call about ten,
But then I've heard that again and again.
You said you'd call about noon,
Well, I knew that was too soon.

Once you said I'll ring you at two,
Yeah, right, I thought, boo hoo.
Broken promises and broken dates,
One's bad, the other I truly hate.

If only you knew this about me.
the time doesn't matter, it's free.
Your call is the important aspect,
Because it makes love grow into respect.

So when you say I'll call you at four,
Please know that as much as I would adore
to hear your voice then or any time,
And that you would call is divine.

Your call is what is important to me,
As it fills my heart with glee
And unleashes it to be free
To live in a world of reality.

For of all the numbers in this world,
Or all the calls your life might hold,
That your call to me takes priority,
Takes me one step closer to my fantasy.

The Difference

Women have a figure,
Men have a build.

Women demand more vigor,
Men settle for a shield.

Women show emotion,
Men hunger for devotion.
Women like convention,
Men strive for invention.

Women seem of good taste,
Men hasten to the chase.
To believe what you hear
Is to think there is a difference my dear.

To believe what you read
Is to deny what you need.
To fly in the face of consensus
Is to get the attention of my senses.

It could be our secret between you and me
Or better yet, it could be for the world to see.
There is no difference, no anomaly
There is only you and me, the meld of harmony.

Some choose to call it symbiotic,
Some may even call it idiotic.
I think of you as no different from me.
I think of you as you and me as me.
For then I know that both of us are free.

The Dream of Life

Goodnight my love for I must sleep.
Awake my heart for I must dream.
Tonight you unleashed my emotions.
Tonight you earned my devotions.
My dream will follow the path to you.
So be gentle and kind and I'll always be true.

The Flower Rooted in my Heart

Oh darling, darling, my sweet darling,
I think of you even as I kneel and pray.

You are the flower that has taken roots in my heart
We have just met but I find it hard to part.

If you were a daisy
Life would not be so hazy.
You love me, you love me not,
Your petals would unfold the plot.

But now to find if there is love in us
I must look into my heart and trust
That what I see is truly real.
And if you are there it is the truth I feel.

The Geneva Convention Rules of Love

We have all heard of the Geneva Convention Rules of War.
That's where a bunch of jokers from our civilized nations got
together and basically said we can't be mean to each other.

Oh, we can blow off each other's heads.
Sever each other's limbs, shatter the other guys to smithereens,
But don't be mean to each other.

Blow off the other guy's head,
But don't punch him in the nose.
Use weapons of mass destruction and blind him,
But don't stick your finger in his eye.

Cut off his arms with shrapnel and gunfire but don't
Punch him in the arm or kick him in the shins.
Gas him and paralyze him or even blow away his insides,
But don't hit him below the belt.

Surround his army, isolate them and starve them to death,
But you must feed them three meals a day when you control them.

Imagine these jokers getting together at a place in Switzerland
Because it was classified as neutral,
And writing these rules of civility.

It's like the opposing mafia bosses meeting over a sumptuous dinner
At some lavish hotel. They are not allowed to bring their guns
To the meeting, just chatting away to set up their own rules of behavior.

Has anyone heard of, or even thought about
The Geneva Convention Rules of Peace? Do they exist?
I'm afraid not. Rules that would say that nations must
Respect each other, not wage war on another and
To just mind their own business.

Rules of peace where the weapons of mass destruction would consist
Of waging love and getting to know each other with the intent
Of enjoying each other and having a good time.

Then the armies of that conflict would be tourists and travelers
Visiting each other's countries; sightseeing and enjoying the
Friendships and love that would be thrown at them.
And in turn extending invitations to the other nation's people to
Visit them with the intent of surpassing the hospitality they received.

No, by the present rules that would be too simple, too civil.
No blood could be shed. No lives could be ruined.
It wouldn't be allowed to kill or maim the other person.
It would be just too friendly, too loving.
No, under the present rules of conduct, that just wouldn't work.
But wouldn't it be great if it did?

The Journey of Two Hearts

My love's character is a beautiful innocence whose light glows
Casting shadows of temptations dancing on the walls of my soul.

Its journey's path is paved with the cobblestones of good intentions
And thundered over by the wild hooves of desire and indiscretions.

The twisting, curving path's swirling dust
Is settled by the tears of wanting and the sweat of lust.

Reaching its climactic end at the golden arches of submission,
Just as the wild ride was about to take on a new direction.

Now our union is cemented by the sacred vows
Of two lives melding into one, for all the world to know.

Whose journeys now embark on the never ending quest of happiness.
With embracing hearts and silent sighs to never again feel loneliness.

The Last Journey

Promise yourself before your last rest
To accomplish those things that would make your life the best.
Try to follow the rules of life,
To love and cherish and hold dear to you
All the things that one needs to be complete.

For then as you look out on life's horizon
And you see the glow of your life setting
Like a distant sun that takes with it
The memories and events of a life complete,
A life that glows even brighter for all the good you've done.

And you see on life's sea the reflection
of a golden carpet ending at your feet.
For that is the path you laid out for yourself.
As you walk it for all the world to see.

The Laws of Physics

How can I measure my love for you,
How can it be described or defined?

Can it be measured on a scale of power or pull of force
Or weighed on a balance against all the world's mass?

Or compared to all the beauty the world has ever known
Can it be defined by all the words known to man
Or described by all the languages of mankind?

It would take all the music written to produce its score
all the world's flowers blooming just to describe its core.

I am human and life for me is finite and jade
But my love for you will never die, will never fade.

If it were a marathon it would never cease
Or if emitting light would outshine the stars with ease.

How best can I describe its strength, its mass,
Can it be compared with anything that has come before?

Can it be held in check until my feelings pass
Or unleashed at its source to explode and devour?

No, but like all laws of nature it has its
Equal, its balance of power.
My only hope in preserving my mind and my heart I can see
Is that my love for you is in
Balance with your love for me.

The Lure of Love

I feel your heart beating within mine.
As your soul clutches me to its breast.
And with every tick of the clock
While sharing ourselves we unlock
The secret and the truly real test
That what we have is divine.
Just two souls together on this earth
Enjoying each other for all we are worth.
And our waking thoughts become so pure
We are not separated even in our dreams.
For our love for each other is the lure
Cast into the middle of life's stream.
Attracting each to each in life and in our dreams.

The Magical World of You

Countless stars sparkle from your eyes
Enough to start an entire galaxy.

The warm loving sun shines from your heart
Strong enough to warm my soul when we are apart.

A moonlight glow radiates from your sleep
Lying beside you envelopes me oh so deep.

Your touch is the cool silky breeze
Swirling over my body to place my life at ease.

Lilting concertos flow from your voice

Capturing all my senses as I have no choice
But to live my life in the mystical world of you
Jealously clutching all your secret powers so true.

As I choose not to share them with anyone
Because they fill my life to make me the chosen one.

The Paradox of Anticipation

My thoughts are full of anticipation
But they require your participation.

At times I am so selfish
But then you can be so devilish.

I've placed you on a throne
With my world at your feet,
Even though you want to be alone
And know for every victory there is a defeat.

Every queen must have her court,
I offer you my heart in last resort.
I look upon you as majesty,
Though it may seem a travesty.

At night when I murmur your name
My heart flickers and bursts into flame.
My heart tells me to capture her,
But my heart says to defer.

I want to act with conviction,
But do you really want addiction?
So I say let us be, let's sit back and see
What life has in store for us,
For it may only be a ride on a bus.

But if the stops are as I anticipate
Then the ride is one in which we must participate.

The Poem That I Crave

Write a poem just for me.
It could be one line or two or even three.
The lines don't need to rhyme or even make sense
But I will know that it belongs to me and no one else.

It could be light and terse
With only one verse
Like a sparrow flitting from branch to branch in a tree.
Or like an eagle in the sky flying so free and so high
Circling its vast domain of space
All the while its eye on what it seeks to possess.

It can be just one word that would in itself define
All the feelings welled up that are mine.
All my hopes and dreams that could be set free.

That magical word poem could be
Your name or just you
As it defines what I crave and desire
What I want forever and ever
And set my whole life on fire.

Or my poem could be just one syllable or even one letter
Just one letter of the alphabet
But oh what it could be
As I will know it is meant for me.

That one letter could be for instance "I"
I'll fill in the rest and then our love can do the rest.
I love you, I need you, I want you just for me.

That one letter poem will capture my mind and be
Keeper of my thoughts and reveal
The bountiful love stored inside of me.

From one letter to one word,
from one word to one line,
From one line to one verse,
Our love will grow and be heard.

From this world in our universe
As our love floats in the clouds to traverse,
All the paths the angels take
On their way to earth for joy to make.

For people like you and me
Who are blessed and can see
That what we have is oh so real
And what we share the world should feel.

The Puzzle of Us

Why am I so hard to explain
And you so difficult to understand?
We both speak the language
And both read the written word.
Could it be the unspoken word
And maybe the unwritten phrase?

If you could read my heart
Or listen inside me to my thoughts,
Listen to my silent prayers,
Feel the teardrops falling on my soul
And be so sure of my thoughts and love
To gain the confidence as of your own.

This cannot come from just wanting
And us hoping that by chance
The pieces of this puzzle will fit together
To reveal a picture of contentment.

The test of our differences
Is likened to the granule of sand
Nurtured by the oyster through time
To reveal its pearl for all to see.

Ours must be a mutual love
A mutual need that seems immortal,
That can only be satisfied forever
By the unselfish giving of our souls.

The Resounding Spiritual Score

Many days have come and gone
Years and seasons just flow along
But I ask what is lacking in my life
What do I need to be complete?

Is it lack of achievement or doing,
Must my life be marked by achieving?
Are there possessions I should crave?
Or places to visit of which they rave?

Are there masterpieces of art to view
Or literature to be read and pondered anew?
Is it that poem I should create
Or the song I need compose to relate?

Yes, there are worldy things to ponder
And spiritual feelings upon to wonder
But the real test of my absolution
Is to secure your love as the solution.

Your love will make me king of all worldly things
And allow me to transcend all spiritual thinkings
My every thought would then be encircling your soul.
My every word a part of a master score.
The touch of your lips the sweet nectar of gods,
The press of your body for what I long.

Then as the days come they would not go
But remain with me to accumulate more.
A resounding spirited piece to become a symphonic score
Of love and hope and pleasures
To be shared with you forever more.

The Saying of Grace

Some of us look to You, Our Lord
Others look to a Spirit from within
And others may choose to believe
in what they know.

But if there is one common belief in
this little group gathered here,
It is that we believe in family
and friends whether far or near.

We thank our lucky stars for those feelings so old
And count our blessings like a
miner counts his gold.

Food and joy and drink make this
a celebration,
But it is family and friends that
give us realization.

That our lives are filled with love and caring,
Whose seeds are scattered by the
winds of sharing
As we meet more friends we can embrace
and love
Beyond this little group on which
You smile from above.

The Stars Above Sing Our Song

It was just a little note you sent to me
But oh what that note turned out to be.
It was a greeting you passed on to me
"The stars above sing your song."

It was then I knew deep in my heart.
Something more was about to start.
A little piece of me
Fell in love
With a little piece of you
and validated why I think of you
The whole day through.

That little note became a prophecy
And made real my secret fantasy.
It unleashed the colors in my heart
To paint a picture of magical art.

It put me on this fluffy cloud of happiness
And from the picture in my heart I knew
You could end my loneliness.
I long to hold you in my arms and
As I fathom all your charms,
Whisper to each other that all along
The stars above are singing our song
And that we were meant to be
For I was meant for you
And you were meant for me.

The Thought of You

I love the thought of you
And know what I ought to do.

My heart says to take you back,
My mind tells me what you lack.

I should have known all along
Your type is no different than a song.

When the music is playing
And the party is swaying,

All seems so exciting
All seems so inviting.

But when the music stops
And the curtain drops

You go off the stage
I'm left alone in rage.

You're off with another Johnny-come-lately
I'm alone drowning in sorrow daily.

You put my body on the rack,
My mind you send to hell and back.

I hide behind the curtain
so the world won't see my burden.

I love the thought of you,
But can my heart survive this blue.

Can my heart learn to love another again?
Or am I destined to love you to the end?

The Trail Between Two Hearts

He met her at the dance
She stood out like a beacon
Shining a cool low glow.

WILLIAM MIJO GRANICH

Holding her while dancing
Was like the world one could never know.

The words were plentiful with promises of more.
each phrase measured as set to an
arrangement of a musical score.

And as they touched and their bodies
brushed
They felt the exciting rush of their
bodies thrust
Swaying in sync and pulsing to
the rhythm of lust.

And so it was when the last dance was done
They parted to a lonesome tune of longing
And trusting fate to do the right
thing for their belonging.

Fate did deal its hand to arrange a
moonlit dinner.
Under sparkling silver stars
A setting that could lead to promised paradise.
They enjoyed each other even more than before
And as the evening went on they both knew
they would enjoy it even more.

Soon he was holding her in his arms
Feeling her warm and tender body and
loving all her charms.

Tight little body, just a wisp
of a thing.
Holding her, his heart beckoning.

As love progressed he could hardly
imagine such beauty lying there
And he knew
paradise was about to unfold.

Her supple body like curves and trails
Taking him from here to the world
of ecstasy
Curves and trails and gentle hills
With a peak or valley now and then.

Linger here, rest there, no hurry
to find the end.
One trail great, another better yet.
One trail leading to bliss
Another to sheer contentment
And still another with promises of more.

Cool off and rest, enjoy the journey
at each bend
All the while hoping their travels
that night would never end.

It's been a while since and he
knows the trails from end to start
But that doesn't mean he travels them
with closed heart.
His travels are in open amazement
for now they're never apart
And their journey includes the trail
between their hearts.

The Trail of Love

I never knew
Anyone in the world
Like you.

From the firm mounds
Of your breasts,
Through the valleys
Of the rest,
I can now plot my course
For the travels over our
Love trails.

Your reactions to my touch
Launch me to journeys such,
My days and nights
Are reserved
For the sensations
Of you.

We can now float

Among the stars.
Or descend to tumble
On the bed of roses
That is ours.

I now have you
To hold on to.
Please, don't let go.
Hold on to me.

The Trails of my Memories

When I'm alone at night and
    the room goes dark
I wander the trails of my memories.

You appear. I close my eyes
    and we're alone in my memories.
Everything is so clear, so true
    to life.
Except why did we break up?

As I'm deep in the trails of my memories
I'm startled by a screech of a car that
    sounds like a baby's cry.

Now it's clear why we broke up.

I stare at the dark and see reality.

I wanted only you and me, no
    sharing you with anyone.
You saw beyond, you saw the
    future with child and family.

Now I'm alone in the dark and
    know who was wrong and who was right.
There is no you and me.
You have your life, your child
    and family,
While I'm alone in the dark, wandering
    the trails of my memories.

POEMS AND PROSE

The Tree of Life

When I was caught up in the living and strife
I had no time to think of what was beginning
To be an awareness of the trimming
Of the tree of life.

The intricate entwinement of my needs and dreams
Strung around the tree of existence that was life
As sure as day followed day
I was marching to a tune I thought O.K.

Now as I become aware there is more to life
I can go on trimming the tree of life.
As the lights come on one string at a time
the dreams that shine out are all mine.

For every dream, for every wish I stored within me
I find they are now flowing and longing to be freed.

My tree is being trimmed and displayed for all to see
With the source of power that only you can provide for me.

You are my child, my friend,
My companion, my soul sister, my mate.
You are my today, my tomorrow,
My lover, my all, my fate.

The Truth 1

Truth is like a huge ringing bell
Heard by all the same its clear knell.
And those who argue its tone
Cannot alter it to their own.
Those who want to alter its tone
In time will find themselves alone.
And even those away from its sound
Know that its ringing abounds.

The Truth 2

Truth cannot be fabricated because
by the laws of nature it exists as an element in itself.

And though you cannot fabricate
the pure elements of oxygen and hydrogen,
they can be combined to form water,
a fabricated compound.
But when that is broken down reveals the elements of itself.

Untruths are fabrications of imaginations
and alterations of facts.
And at times sprinkled with some
truths for guise or effect.

But as water is always water
so then is a lie always a lie.

The Truth 3

We recycle matter, objects and things.
Whole industries are devoted to such endeavors.

But who recycles the truth,
distills it and cleanses it to be more pure and omnipotent.

Certainly not those politicians who are self-serving
and at times grind the truth into dust to be thrown into
the eyes of their followers so they
can show them a path more chosen by them.

Or paid agents whose advertisements use the truth that is
slanted and bent to better sell their wares.

Or those who don't know the value of truth
and contaminate it to suit their own needs.

No, the truth needs not be processed and filtered.
But if it does undergo a process of investigation and reason in a person's mind,
It will emerge strengthened and clean as the pure truth in itself.

The Way It Is

Can you feel the sunset in the sky?
Brush the stars with your eyes?
Can you hear the flowers close their blooms at night?

See the puppies grow even before their mother knows?

I can hear your every thought,
Feel your pain before it starts.
Miss your smile before it's gone,
Hear your laugh before it starts.

Can you touch my love and hold it in your hands?
Or weigh it on a scale?
Hear my teardrops fall?
Or measure my love because it's real?
Can you hear the music before it starts?
Or sing the chorus before it's known?
Return before you're even gone
Or climb the mountain that's not there?

Well, my love, I'm burdened with those traits.
Beholden to you even when you're not at your best.
So please my love, let me take this cross
And set it down so I can rest.

The World at Peace

From the heat of battle
Through the scars of war

Hear the swords rattle
Fear the scars more

Brave men have fought
What negotiations have wrought
War is such drastic travail
Logic must always prevail
Why can't nations concede
That negotiations could succeed

And battles would not be waged
If the negotiators engaged

Were chosen from the battle line
And then given enough time

To put aside their differences
And discuss their preferences

WILLIAM MIJO GRANICH

Living in a world at peace
Is the goal we must reach

For then joy and happiness
Will be everyone's heritage.

They Must Fill The Need

His sword was angry
Its sheath bare
His heart was heavy
Yet filled with care.

The anger was in check
But his resolve you could detect
He was at the ready
His composure ever steady.

He knew what his task
Evil was to be unmasked
Wrong was to be abhorred
No need to ask for more.

There is always a price to pay
And no matter what the cost
Or the lives to be lost
Right was to be sorted from disarray.

Who are these dichotomies of repute
the ones asked to settle disputes?
Who are these lads and lasses
Who rise up from the masses?

They are the ones of resolute
Known as heroes absolute.

Thinking and Dreaming

Lately I've had this hollow feeling
I kept thinking and dreaming of what I was missing.
Various things came to the fore,

Even things I never thought of before.

Was it food or music, a book or wine?
Was it something I missed for a long, long time?
Was it something I never had before,
Fame, or fortune, a new romance or more?

Or could it be I knew all the time,
Something I knew before I made up my mind?
My thoughts were peeled away layer by layer
With each new surface seeming clearer and clearer.
Like a child unwrapping a gift in a frenzied whirl,
Or an oyster giving the ultimate to surrender its pearl.

With all my discarded thoughts lying at my feet,
The passion in my thinking was for our hearts to meet,
To be connected and bonded by ties so strong,
To unravel and break them would be so wrong.

So now I know without even thinking,
What I miss is you, awake or dreaming.
You were meant for me as I for you,
So let's bond our hearts in a love that's true.

Three Wise Men and Me

A wise man once said to me as I recall
There were three of them you know,
No not the ones who rode the camels, no not at all
this was one of three wise men
From my home town of Bruneau.

My home town near the tracks where ponies run around.
Only ponies run there and camels never do
'Cause there's no sand or even palm trees anywhere around.

Oh, and you should know
I never even knew a man who rode a camel
Let alone a wise man who rode a camel or ponies you see.

And also I can't say any wise men I did know
Besides these three I'm talking about.

And sometimes in their wiseness
I have doubt
What with living in Bruneau and all that snow.

As you can guess the snow in winter was not too wise to take.

But enough of that, I digress.
Well, anyway this wise man,
One of three, said to me
Bet the line and put it
On Wise Manarunnin' in race three.

I never knew what bet the line did mean.
But he was the wise man
And I'm sure his mind was keen.
He's going off at five to one and can't miss –
Or did he tell me one to five,
And those odds were his?

Well whichever it would be
I was to put my money on the one he told me.
So early that day I rode the train to the track in town
Got in line but was way way back.
All the while clutching my C-note against my chest
Figurin' how I would spend my winnings at their best.

Barely made the window as it was about to close
And was lucky to get my money down
When I heard the bell a'clanging
And the crowd all noise did drown
The roar of "they're off and running"
Was music to my ears as my heart was churning.

Standing at the rail waiting for the ponies to pass.
Heading for the finish line
Them making noise and dust as they run on down.
The first that passed didn't look familiar to me,
Or the second or third or fourth or any I could see.
No red striped shirt on the rider of Wise Manarunnin' appeared to me.

Then somewhere in the rear of the pack it was plain to see
Was the one the wise man touted on to me.
Didn't look like he could come up to the lead in time,
In fact he finished so far back he was dead last.
It's then I recalled what the wise man said to me.

If he don't break the finish line at least three lengths free,
You'll be all the wiser and that I guarantee
'Cause this race will have been just a tune-up you see,
And the next one, well just get all your money down
He's going to cross the finish line
Ahead of all these clowns.

So the next week in the race he did run
Went off on odds of one hundred to one,
And that's the race he also never won.

Well needless to say it's now known
There was a wise man in my town, but also a clown.
One doesn't need many clues to figure it and to know
That from then on to now I'm known
Around the town as Bozo.

Ticitsa Koha Nije Pjeiroala

Kad goru Millitse
Slatka non je pjesmitsa

Sve se coupe ticitse
Okolo mala Millitse

Sve ticitsa iz gore
Poletile na more

Samo jedna ostala
Koja nije pjevala

Bidna mala ticitse
Udruzlie mala Millitse

Toast #1

A dash of friends.
A splash of spirits.

Mix with food and music and conversation.

The recipe for the good life.

Toast #2

We've journeyed from near and far,
Some friends from yesterday,
Some friends from today.
What matters most is who we are.

We pray tomorrow's tears be soft,
And our laughs deep from our hearts.

Today is here,
Let tomorrow bring no fear.

Way Out

The spaceman's conversation after capturing the earth's spacecraft and interrogating its crew:

"These earthlings seem like intelligent beings except this one who's ranting and raving about 20 million somethings, and that he wants a refund. I don't understand him. What's a refund? Does it have anything to do with what our leader says about the shaft they gave him? I didn't think a shaft had any value. He must be loony, but he does sing a mean song."

What Do They Know

Scholars and scientists and theologians all agree
Life began eons ago long before you and me.
But we know better and have proved them wrong
And that I'm certain of as the day is long.

The big bang occurred last night at about half past two
When you rolled over and whispered to me I love you.

It was then our brand new galaxy was formed.
A brand new galaxy that was to become our toy
In which our hearts could travel filled with joy.
Zooming from planet to planet among the stars
Our very own Venus and Saturn, Pluto and Mars.

Just now and then touching on earth to rest
And we knew our love was passing its final test.

For the next hour as our galaxy was explored
And events happened that romantics put into song,
I whispered to you at about half past three,
I love you every bit as much as you love me.

What I Need To Know

Heavy hangs the burden of life,
Mystery shrouds the purpose of strife.

Within myself I need to know,
Are these chambers or vaults or dungeons of sorrow?

Are they dark rooms or cathedrals of joy?
Are they places of torture
Or settings for the purpose of nurture?

Could they exist within the walls of my heart
Or maybe in the halls of my soul?

Your love controls this mystery for me,
Your love is the key to set me free.

Show me the key, unlock the mystery.
Open the door, let the light shine on me.
Breathe life into me as you set me free,
And I will love you even beyond eternity.

What The World Should Know

At Christmas eve I feel sorry
for the trees not sold,
Standing cold and lonely on the
empty lot that looks so dark
and old and they don't know.

And at the pound I feel sorry
for the puppies that go unadopted
but still wag their tails 'cause

they don't know.

And when I walk the streets at
night and in a dark alley a kitty
meows for a friend it doesn't know.

Ot when I'm alone and cold and lonely
in my bed I feel the pangs of love
for someone I don't know.

If all the lonely things and creatures
in this world were matched with what
they deserve to know

Peace and joy and love
would abound for all the
world to know.

Whispers Become Thoughts

When first we met
I wondered what our words really meant.
The vowels so clear,
The sounds so near,
Yet the meanings so unclear.

So unsure the tales of lonely lives
and empty arms
Of useless tasks and wasted us.

I wondered if they were said to draw
us near and sooth our fears.
Or serve as a sandy beach upon which
to walk holding hands and caring for us.

Then in our many strolls and all
the embraces
Our words became whispers and
Our lives started to clear.
and as our whispers turned
to thoughts, our thoughts became
what we could hear.
Thoughts beyond words and whispers.
Thoughts that blend our lives

and give us meaning
And make us two into a greater one.

Who We Are

I understand when you misinterpret who I am.
I don't mind when you doubt my real intentions.
I don't even wonder why you misread my intentions,
For as I analyze all this I have a better understanding of who I really am.

I know you for your actions.
I know you for your words.
But the logic of words can come from a misinformed heart
and may even fall on deaf ears.

But our advantage is speaking the language of the heart.
And hearing the unspoken sounds of love,
And knowing deep inside the
feelings of the heart will sustain us throughout the years to come.

Why Can't We Be a Part of Me

The thoughts of you are with me constantly
You are in my brain, a part of me.

My memories of you are like a rose's scent
I cup it to my face and breathe in sheer content.

I close my eyes and your face appears.
I open my heart and you I visualize.

I dream of the time I saw you from far away,
And scheme of the moment I'll hold you as mine.

The sunlight streaming through your flaxen auburn hair,
The moonlight gleaming off your body bare.

Our arms entwined and holding tight
Our bodies pressed so close in utter delight.

What torture I create, for you belong to another,
I'm sentenced to suffer your absence forever.

My longing for you is so dark and blue and true
the thoughts of you are with me constantly.

The pain I feel is such a sweet, sweet drain,
The suffering for you I endure again and again.

I can only dream of what might have been
If you were mine and we a part of me.

Why Him, Not Me

He's playing the part of a fool
And at times even a clown.
While I sit home and seem so cool
Alone in my sorrow and drown.

He has the pleasure of your company,
He has the run of your house.
While I feel like a louse.
I'd rather be near you, even as a mouse.

I'd risk the wrath of Murph the kitty
Just to be with you on your turf.
For even Murphy would take pity on me
And let me stay there as company.

For this to go on much longer
My heart must be much stronger.
End this torture of me,
End this misery I plead.

I want to be the one at your side,
The one in which you can confide.
I want to again feel like a man,
So please my dear, incorporate my plan.

Wild Unbridled Love

My love runs wild
Riding bareback
On the crazed stallion of lust

Its thighs warmed
By the sweaty flanks
Of the flames of desire

The pulsing, throbbing, syncopated thrust
fills my heart
With the surging blood of your love.

It charges over the clover covered fields
Of prayers answered and promises kept
Riding headlong through the misty walls
Of broken dreams and broken vows.

Riding and charging and hurtling
To the crescendo and staccato
Of my heart's craving and demanding

When will it tire, when will it ease
Where will it end, where will it cease

When you are mine. When you are mine. When you are mine.

Willie's Revolutionary New Idea

Willie was a normal kid nearin'
eighteen and had his pride.
Could get a date quickerin' the
other ones especially if he tried.
Mostly though the girls would give
him no never mind,
Especially when he tried to undress them
he had no luck of any kind.

Then on one date with the day
turnin' to night,
Musta been by accident his britches fell out of sight.
Fell clean on down around his
ankles and kinda tight.
Shown him in the flesh from his naked
waist on down.

Him standin' there naked as the day he was born'd
But to his surprise his date showed more amusement than fright
Right then and there Willie had

a revelation, amen.
Turned out to be easier undressin'
hisself instead of them
And would you figure it they
didn' seem to mind at'all.

From then on his usual date would
start full clothes on him,
then do his thing and go as far as possible could.
One clothes at a time lookin'
for a win.
All the while makin' small talk
like all OK,
Hopin' they'd not catch on where he
was a headin' or carin' what he'd say.

But he know'd it all along and kept
on a thinkin' this time it's gonna work.
They probabled wondered what the
hell is this about.

Don't seem natural him not grabbin'
at them and so they'd had their doubt
But iff'n they did catch on some
would do a double take,
Others actin' like they'd saw'd a lil' ol' snake.
And some goshalmighty fearin'
like they saw'd a big ol' snake.

And no never mind which way the
date would end,
Willie didn' care much as before
or his conscious bend.
Just put on his clothes, take
them home and fold up his tent.

This new revolutionary idea worked
real good, too.
He wouldna tell his buddies
cause he knew
This new idea was hissin'
and it worked better than a kiss'n
He did just real fine until this one time
Which was the last time and
that he truly figured.

This one time he prepared to do
his thing in front of Kathleen.
Did it just on the edge of the woods
which was in the park near town.
She was alone sunnin' herself
enjoyin' the heat and the breeze
Willie came up on her, she layin'
on her back at ease.
Her head arestin' on this
beach chair.
Just a half chair she used at the beach when alone
'Cause it was easier to shake
off the sand when fixin' to go home.

Willie seen her eyes mostly closed,
Worked right up to her a reach away.
Had no idea what he was
gonna say.
Figured his new idea was leadin' him
all the way.

WILLIAM MIJO GRANICH

His private actin' like a divining rod
Not lookin' for water
Just glad she was takin' a nod.

Well just then Kathleen opened
wide her eyes.
Musta liked what she saw
and to Willie's surprise,
Grabt aholt of that divining rod
in one cast
Talk about a snake her reach
was just as fast.
By now she mostly sittin' up
and pullin' his private to herself.

Willie so scair't and he didn't
want to go along,
Had to though or his private
would have gone hisself.

By the time Willie was
near her cheek
She upped and let go so's
to grab his naked behind.
There's opportunities in
life that present themselves
for us to take,
And this was one Willie would
not pass up for heaven's sake.

He spun his naked behind
half way around.
Jumped straight up so's could
have set the record for the
highest jump in town.
Landed in a heap four, five yards away.
Come up runnin', his feet
pumpin' like pistons against the ground.
His clothes lay behind a tree he passed
But to gather them was the last
thought he had.
just get out of there and make it
real, real fast.

'Bout a quarter mile in the woods
had to stop to catch his breath.
Sat there on his bare bottom
his back aleanin' on a tree.
Settin' there awaitin' for the
time to pass
So's could go back and fetch
his shirt and pants
And hopin' Kathleen was gone,
just took her chair and went on home at last.

So now when they pass on the
street in the light of day
No more revolutionary new
ideas abound.
'Cause they ain't even worth
throwin' away.
Kathleen always a coy smile
on her face.
Willie just plain business
lookin' the other way.
All the while glad and thankin'
the Lord there's people all around.

Willows and Cards

You can bend me, bend me baby,
    but you won't break me.
You can plot and plan and scold,
    do all the things of old,
Do all the things my love lets you do,
Do all the things to split us in two.

It's as though we're playing this game of cards.
A real life game with a hand dealt by the Gods.
Spades are trump, but why not hearts?
You bid, I pass, but it doesn't matter if we're apart.

You can break my heart with threats that we should part.
Threats meant to drain the passions from my heart.
And when my tear drops fall when we are apart
And lie at rest on the branches in my heart
The winds rustling through my sadness

Test my love even more than madness.

Wishes

I wish that you would think of me
as I think of you.
I wish that you would long for me
as I long for you.
I love your looks, your being and
the way you look at me.
I love your presence but am lonely
at your absence
I love your handling of life
especially if it would involve me.
Having you would be like a parched
traveler in the desert
Going from oasis to oasis, thirsting at
each for that cup of cool water.
Traveling the journey that ends with you
in my arms,
Our bodies entwined, your lips
just mine.
The heartbeat heard indistinguishable
between yours and mine
Forever and ever and ever
        to the end of time.

Wondering

Have you ever wondered why the mustang is free
To run the plains so wild and bold?
Have you ever wondered why the thoroughbred
Is not so free but harnessed even as a colt?

In the rain forest flowers grow wild
And spread their seed among the trees,
While in the shop the orchid is cultured
And tilled to grow in pots for all to see.

And why are pop songs played until they die,
Yet classics live to bring tears to the eye?

Thoroughbred, let the mustang loose in you.
Orchid, let your beauty bloom and spread its hue.
Soprano, fill the air with your classic melody,
Fill the world with what only you can do to me.

Let me be the plain over which you run wild.
Let me be your rainforest and show you are not a child.
Let me hear your song of life, your lilt not strife.
For only then can you be you,
And only then will we be free.

Words One Could Regret

Words are cheap unless spoken in anger
Then they could be costly and the price no longer
A price one is willing to pay so readily,
But a price that takes its toll like a medley

Of regrets and hurts, of tears and feelings fractured.
so think before you speak in anger
And you'll not regret the feelings you manufacture.

Words

There are countless words in our language,
The dictionary is just chock full of them.
Books are written with their various arrangements.
Some tell of peace, others of anguish.
Some must be said and be heard.
Others should be left in silence instead.

But the ones with most meaning
Are those wrapped around our feelings.
Some just run through our heads
Others demand to be said.
At times silence is golden
Then there are those that must be spoken.

In a contract of law they have official status.
Under a moonlit sky their effect is to move us.
Words that describe tales of the heart

Are used to convey feelings when we are apart.
Some are written and put in a song.
Others are used to tell what is wrong.

And when words spoken are foreign
They still mean the same no matter the origin.
Cavemen on their walls carved hieroglyphics
Then words later translated them to specifics.
Words can describe puffs of smoke used as signals
Right from the wild west to ecclesiastical windows.

And where would we be if we didn't know
That one was by land and two was by sea?
And words that apply to life and so describe
Are more lasting and better than those that deride.
But those that are the most moving involve love
And come sacred as though written from above.

Pure written words like: "I love you, I truly do.
Please love me for I surely love thee"
Are the ones that make this world go around.
And as much fun as on a merry-go-round.

You are My Camelot

Today I did a lot,
Today I visited Camelot.

Today was a good day for me,
today I planted a tree.

The simple things bring me pleasure,
It's those basic things I treasure.

So many thoughts are in my head,
I hesitate to go to bed.

For I'd lie there alone and borrow
Even more thoughts from tomorrow.

But then I think and think and scheme
And wonder if I could meet you in my dream.

I close my eyes and visualize

You by my side, you tantalize.

So slowly, oh so slowly I let go
And reach out to meet your glow.

Tonight I'm going to do a lot,
Tonight I'm going to visit Camelot.

You Are My Journey

Just like the light that shines from the sun
And melts the night to say a new day has begun,
My life started the day we met.
All the days before I can forget.

You are the one with all the charms.
Little wonder I can't sleep without you in my arms.

Everybody was meant for somebody.
Everybody needs someone to love.
You are now the reason for me,
Loving you is like it was meant to be.

Without you life would have no meaning.
My journey would have no ending.
Everybody needs someone to love,
I need you to have my journey done.

You are My Ninth Wave

The times we are together
I want us to go on forever.
Your warmth and conversation
Fill me with warm anticipation.

It's like the waves all surfers seek,
The ones that go on forever toward the beach.
Their crests are endless in their flow,
As they swallow the sand row on row.

Surfers that are in the know
Seek the ninth wave for the show.

WILLIAM MIJO GRANICH

Higher and stronger and longer in flight,
Like the stars riding the clouds at night.

With you at my side,
My heart is ready for that ride
To distant and exotic places
That only one in love faces.

When our cheeks do brush
And our lips are about to touch,
I feel a warm and burning desire,
One that sets my heart on fire.

When I see your warm, soft body so divine
When our bodies do entwine,
It's then I feel you are all mine
And I ride that romantic wave
Feeling I am no longer to life a slave
To life's harsh demands,
To society's many commands.
And as my wave crests toward the shore
I know it's you whom I adore.

But when that wave breaks
And dissipates in foam on the sand,
My heart seems to follow in its wake
My life is again alone and bland.

Just like when we're apart,
It takes a toll on my heart.
You never call to say hello
Or to tell me all is mellow.

It's as though you never think of me,
Unless I'm there for you to see.
I'm alone and lonely in my bed,
Having left so many things unsaid.

Being alone and lonely at night
I think of all the things you made right.
I count all your many charms
And wish that you were in my arms.

My heart is weighted with sweet sorrow,
But sleep will help usher in tomorrow.
When my mind is no longer like jello,
And the tears lie dry upon my pillow.

So enchanting as you may be
and though you may not always think of me,
I'll paddle out to catch that ninth wave,
And ride it all the way to shore.
Hoping you'll think of me so brave,
You'll want me to surf right to your door.

You are My Senses

You are the flower that has taken roots in my heart.
The flower that is nourished with tears because we are apart.
We were the couple all noticed as we walked away,
Now I sit alone in the diner as the crowd passes and I must stay.

My life that once was the envy of all our friends
Is now covered with gossip that seems never to end.

Once at the end of each exciting day
My clothes were hung and neatly put away.
Now at the end of each lonely day
They lie on the floor all crumpled in total disarray.

When the telephone rang and you were in my life.
My heart would skip a beat in total delight.

Now the ring makes my heart completely stop
Until I learn it is just someone selling a mop.

As the night drags along I lie solitary in bed,
And pray the morning light will take the night and gloom away.
Will my heart ever again be light and fantastical,
And dance to the tune of a light staccato?

Will my eyes ever again see the color of flowers?
Or my ears hear the songs of birds or the raindrops of showers?

Will I ever learn to live without you?
Or will my life forever be only hues of blue?

WILLIAM MIJO GRANICH

You Are The Key to My Fantasy

From the surging of your breasts
As they press against my chest.

The path of love brings out the rest
and we are left at our complete best
With our bodies pressed so tight
We just know that all is right.

With our legs all entwined
Our minds are left to unwind
Our actions reach such resolve
Inhibitions just completely dissolve.
We float on the pure warm clouds of love
Just two angels making love far above.
Why restrict ourselves, we can be selfish
While dancing in the clouds and feel so devilish.

And come back to earth and reality
Only when we book our next flight to fantasy.
For now we have the key to you and me
Hidden away so no one else can see
That what we have others cannot measure
Because we know it is our very own treasure.

You Are the Prize of My Life

I'm just another name in the local phone directory.
You make me feel I'm an aristocrat in the social directory.

I'm just a guy leaning on the rail betting on a nag at the local track in town.
You make me feel like a socialite in a box relaying my wager on the favorite at Churchill Downs.

I'm just a spectator at a bush league game watching my home team play in the local bowl.
You make me feel I'm the owner of the winning team cheering it on to victory in the Super Bowl.

I'm just a guy recalling the tune I heard last night at the local pub, while having a beer.
You make me feel I composed a symphonic melody for the whole wide world to

cheer.

I'm just driving my old car down the highway near town with no destination in mind.
You make me feel like the triumphant driver at a renowned track taking bows with the crowd milling around.

I'm just fishing around at the local pond happy to get a nibble now and then.
You make me feel like the champion bass fisherman landing the prize catch at the world derby for fishermen.

I'm just a guy jogging the hills on a Sunday afternoon with nothing better to do.
You make me feel like I just set the world record at the Olympic marathon venue.

I know when I first met you there was a lot of competition to win your hand.
Guys were coming calling and lining up to court you and show you the town.

But with all those achievements and all those laurels I imagined too,
I did a whole lot better than my imagination could ever do, because I won you.

You Be The Guide

If you meet one who cannot love
Look on it as a challenge from above.
Maybe it's for lack of a gene
Or maybe they just can't dream.
Or it could be a black hole
In feelings that were never whole.

Take time to analyze and decipher
It's their emotions you must consider.
If they are worthy of more
Show them how to open the door.

There's a vast expanse of life out there
Fresh air and sunbeams for ones that care.
Moonlight and stars they could share
Warm feelings and friendships if they just dare.

Set an example from life you have learned
Be gentle and kind and not taciturn.
Like a young chick they could be
Breaking their shell's constraint
To a whole new world they're
About to enter without restraint.

Let them open their eyes
And their heart will follow
Give them room to stretch
And dream of tomorrow.

Think back to your first love and feelings
Remember how it sent your heart spinning and reeling.
It won't be any different for them
And you can help guide them around the next bend.
And like the path taken by other living creatures and beings
Their journey will be full of promises and good feelings

You Be The Judge And Jury

I abide by the rules of society
I follow the laws as best I can
And the law of double jeopardy
Was written for the good of man
It accounts for the guilty ones
They can't be tried again if convicted once

But why doesn't it apply to me
When my heart is the one on trial
My first conviction was in not meeting you
My sentence was years of loneliness
And the endless time served was my penance

And then when we did meet by chance
My second conviction would be in not having you
And that is beyond the realm of fairness

But I still intend to follow the rules of society
Hoping that you will find the mercy
To not put my heart through the second trial
But be the judge and jury and rule for my survival

You Beautiful, Brilliant, Wild You

You are a dichotomy, a paradox of a
worldly, experienced, beautiful woman
with a brilliant, controllably wild,

exciting mind. You have a genuine
warmth, a glow within that
exhibits a charismatic aura in
your voice, your actions and demeanor.
Yet in a moment you can summon
the little girl in you that can be
both curly ringlet good or mischievous
as her whim dictates.
You are a wild exciting thoroughbred
running through the fields of life
whose warm breezes I feel as you
race by. I'm caught up in the excitement
and promise of life thundering by.
You are portrayed much as the painting
of that ethereal lady hung in the Louvre.
but that is imagination placed on
canvas. You are real, exciting,
omnipresent in all your glory.
how best can I describe my thoughts and assessment of you? I
worship at your feet.
Thoroughbred, run and fly and prance,
live and love and dance. Sweep
the world off its feet as you have
so clearly done to me.

You Changed My World

My concept of the world was different before we met.
I was taught its basics and told that's what is.

But now distance is measured by how far we are apart.
Half the world or half the universe away is based on where you are.
Arm's length in distance is now a true measure
The closeness of our lips is what I treasure.

Beauty was hung on the walls of galleries
For all the world to view.
I now close my eyes and realize
The pure picture of beauty is what I visualize.
Your face, your body, your kindness
Is there in plain view.
No need to pray for more, just review.

Time was defined by the passage of the clock,
For the sun ruled the days and nights.

I now measure time by the moments
We are together or apart.
Eternity, forever, now or never
Is measured by the throbs of my heart.

Holding you is my concept of forever.
think of me as I think of you now and ever.
In each waking moment, in each subconscious thought,
To make my life complete,
I need your love, your all.

You Complete My Learning

My father told me why the birds fly so high –
So to be nearer and nearer to the sky.
My mother told me why the birds always sing –
So to teach the same to their offspring.
My father told me why the trees grow and grow –
To produce lumber for all seeking shelter below.
My mother told me why the trees are so tall –
To shield the birds and animals from dangers they know.

I owe my teachings to those two who gave life to me.
They taught me most of what I needed to know
And allowed me to clearly see
That it wasn't until I met you, my love, my all
That I would learn the meaning of heaven on earth and always recall
That even the nectar of the gods is not as sweet as your love
Nor all the music wrapped into one score and sung from above
Could compare to the melody you lit up inside of me
Or could match your warmth and glow
And that I want the world to know.

You End My Gloom

When I talk with you I sense I'm your friend.
I want us to go on and on and never end.

Then as the hours go by
And there is a void since our last goodbye
Doubt sets in and the world seems to change.
I'm alone with my thoughts hoping

your life is in my range.

Suddenly the phone rings and once again,
The veil of silence is at an end.
Your voice dispels the gloom and doubt,
your words so hit a chord I could shout.

Look at me old world, look at me
    in my relief.
Do you see how I have changed?
I now have a belief.
Look at me critically and carefully.
My life is once again filled
    with tranquility.
Look at me, look at me up and down,
My life no longer seems a merry-go-round.

You I Deserve

Why do the stars shine at night?
Yet they don't shine in the daylight.

I know the sun at night is not there,
But in the sky it is everywhere.

You light up my life in both day and night,
Even when you're not in sight.

I've wondered about these things a lot,
Especially since I met you and you're in my every thought.

Why do I get lost when I'm alone in the woods after dark?
And yet can close my eyes and find you at our bench in the park.

They measure the length of time by the tick of a clock
My measure is how long we are together or apart.

The pangs of hunger tell me when to eat.
My hunger for you is satisfied when we meet.

I've traveled many places and seen all corners of the world.
But in my mind I also remember what I've been told.

As a little boy my mother used to say,

WILLIAM MIJO GRANICH

Live life to the fullest and then some day,

You'll find what you deserve for being so good.
And it's you she was talking about, and I understood.

You Make Me Everything

I am an eagle soaring in the sky.
I am the fearless spy who is not afraid to die.
The consummate skier gliding over virgin snow,
The lead in the greatest Broadway show.

I am the craftiest gambler ever dealt a hand,
The fastest gunslinger in all the land.
I am the field of heather and wild flowers,
I am the one with mystic powers.

I hold the key to life's greatest mysteries.
I dine with kings and queens and royalty.
The surfer who caught the only wave worth waiting for,
The mystery prize behind the correct door.

I am the swiftest predator in the Serengeti.
I am everything that everyone wants to be.
My powers are so far reaching
I can turn a million souls just by preaching.

I am the greatest showman the world has ever known.
I am Houdini and Barnum and Bailey reborn.

I am the craftiest wolf that ever led a pack,
I am the swiftest runner on any track.
I won all the Olympic gold
And hold the secret to never grow old.

The greatest chess player who knows every move,
The artist whose paintings hang in the Louvre.
I am the wind and breeze gliding softly
Through sycamore and alder all so deftly.

The patch of sunlight that turns a gloomy day to Spring,
The world's greatest crooner ever to sing..

Why, why, am I all of the above?
Because, because, I am in love.

You

If I can't be with you and you alone,
I'd feel like a king who lost his throne.

If I can't walk with you at my side
I'd want to sit right down and let the crowd pass by.

Your voice to me is all the songs I've heard,
Your smile more radiant than the stars that glow.

Soil and water and sun cause the plants to grow,
Your smile and touch and caring put my life aglow.

When we dance together and move as one,
The rest of the world become mannequins to me.

The key to my life you somehow hold,
With you at my side I become very bold.

Time stands still and becomes my very own,
My life blooms as a flower you were meant to hold.

If I can't be with you and you alone,
I wouldn't want to be a king even with a throne.

Your Love/My Love

Your love is an eagle soaring
Among the clouds in the sky.

My love is its shadow darting
Over the craggy terrain below.

My love is a lone immigrant
Wading ashore.

Yours a new world embracing me
With love so warm and so complete.

WILLIAM MIJO GRANICH

My love is a lone stalk in
A prairie field of corn.

Your love the prairie enveloping
The world and me.

A lone fish in an ocean so
Broad and deep.

The ocean's schools of fish as far as
One can see.

A lightning bolt illuminating
The sky for a brief moment of me.

A galaxy exploding to form a new world for me to see.

The chiming of a single bell
So distant and alone.

All the world bells ringing
In concert to a harmony of tone.

The final brush stroke on a
Painting to make it complete.

All the paintings of artists and masters
Displayed for the world to see.

A patch of earth to produce
A lone planting.

All the world's earth
To leave us not wanting.

A rose petal tumbling at your feet
And there to lie.

All the world's roses and flowers
That fill the eye.

The breath of fresh air to
Allow me to breathe.

You are all the air for all people
And me to share.

A salute from a lone sentry on duty
In a world destitute.

All the world's armies exalting
An infinite gun salute

A lone diplomat pleading to be
Heard and understood.

The world council of diplomats
Being applauded for their good.

With your love, how can I compete?
How can I share, how do I dare?

Because your love lays
the world at my feet.

My love is tendered pure, simple
And complete.

www.ingramcontent.com/pod-product-compliance
Lightning Source LLC
Chambersburg PA
CBHW061329040426
42444CB00011B/2838